SECRET
ST. AUGUSTINE

A Guide to the Weird, Wonderful, and Obscure

Elizabeth Randall and
William Randall

REEDY PRESS

Reedy Press
PO Box 5131
St. Louis, MO 63139
reedypress.com

Library of Congress Control Number: 2024939301
ISBN: 9781681065687

Design by Jill Halpin

All photos are courtesy of William (Bob) Randall.

We (the publisher and the author) have done our best to provide the most accurate information available when this book was completed. However, we make no warranty, guarantee, or promise about the accuracy, completeness, or currency of the information provided, and we expressly disclaim all warranties, express or implied. Please note that attractions, company names, addresses, websites, and phone numbers are subject to change or closure, and this is outside of our control. We are not responsible for any loss, damage, injury, or inconvenience that may occur due to the use of this book. When exploring new destinations, please do your homework before you go. You are responsible for your own safety and health when using this book.

Printed in the United States of America
24 25 26 27 28   5 4 3 2 1

For Harmony, our fearless daughter,
who included St. Augustine in her list of destinations

View of Castillo de San Marcos
from Matanzas Bay

CONTENTS

ACKNOWLEDGMENTS

First, I would like to thank my husband and travel partner, Bob Randall, for his enthusiasm, support, talent, and companionship in completing this project. Amanda Doyle, my Reedy Press editor, was helpful in answering my questions. Kara Pound of Old City Public Relations did a great job as my publicist. Thanks to Holly Baker of the Florida Historical Society for her stacks of books about St. Augustine history and culture. Thank you to WAG, the Writers Alliance of Gainesville, for bringing Reedy Press to the attention of its members. Thanks to Davey Hartzel and Pete Melfi at 904 Now for bringing my books to the attention of a larger audience. Payson Tilden, Judy Slight, and Julia Delbecchi at the Ximenez-Fatio House are always deserving of my appreciation, especially Julia who doubled as a publicist for two of my speaking events. My gratitude also goes to Gail Phillips of the Lincolnville Museum and Cultural Center who provided civil rights history. Thanks to former City Commissioner Sandra Parks, widow of the late Stetson Kennedy, and former owner of Anastasia Books for her help in identifying St. Augustine "secrets," and answering my questions. Thanks to Monica Edwards, programming coordinator at the St. Johns County Public Library System for giving me a platform. Thank you, Charles Tingley of the St. Augustine Historical Society, for your patient answers to my many questions. The St. Augustine Historical Society always has interesting historical facts for my books, and it would be hard to find a better font of knowledge. Also, its online search engine is one of the best I have ever used. And Bob and I could not have survived without Cameron who plied us with IHOP pancakes during our many visits to the adjoining Days Inn on West 16.

Most of all, thanks to the friendly people of St. Augustine whose pride and love for the ancient city continues without end.

INTRODUCTION

I work as half of a photojournalist team with my husband, Bob. He takes pictures; I write. We have two published books about St. Augustine under our belts, and we thought we knew all there was to know about St. Johns County. We were wrong. There were plenty of secret facts to ferret, weird history to unwind, and uniquely St. Augustine things to undertake (how many cities fire cannons on weekends?). Even though we started our research in 2023 under the blaze of the hottest summer on record, the heat did nothing to deter us from the mysteries inherent in the ancient city.

St. Augustine proudly bears the distinction of being the oldest continuously occupied city in America. It is important for visitors to remember the unique Spanish and British influence on St. Augustine's history, architecture, culture, and customs, a European influence which is inexplicably linked to the ancient city's evolution. The first Spanish period dated from Admiral Menéndez's landing in 1565 until the British took over in 1763. Twenty years later, the British handed St. Augustine back to the Spanish. Thirty-eight years later, Spain ceded colonial occupation to the United States. The ancient city was a US territory until 1845 when Florida became a state.

Most of the sites listed in *Secret of St. Augustine* are free or a minimal cost. From admiring replicas of fine art at Ripley's Believe It or Not!, to hunting haunts in restaurants and museums, to eating ice cream from a recipe originated by World War II bombardiers, St. Augustine has it all: beaches, gourmet dining, concerts, festivals and attractions, and a young and a vibrant business community.

Because it's the oldest continuously occupied city in America with a rich history from the Spanish conquistadors, the British aristocracy, antebellum Americans, and civil rights leaders, it's steeped in secrets. There are stories behind the forts, old Spanish houses, slave market, civil rights landmarks, museums, hotels, art galleries, a college that was once a luxury hotel, and more. These places all have secrets to tell and, since it's St. Augustine, one or two ghost stories as well.

Once you go to St. Augustine, you keep going back. Although it's the oldest city in America, its secrets never get old.

MISSION NOMBRE DE DIOS MUSEUM

What ancient relic of the founder of St. Augustine resides at the mission?

Mission Nombre de Dios translates to *Name of God* in English, and it was the first Franciscan mission in the United States. It was christened by Don Pedro Menéndez de Avilés of the Spanish royal troops, a fierce Catholic, and a subject of Phillip II. Menéndez is considered the founder of St. Augustine, and his casket is available for viewing in the on-site museum.

Ironically, the conquistador did not die in one of the many battles of ancient Florida, but in Spain, helpless and bedridden from typhus, in 1574. A bloodthirsty man of the 16th century, he slaughtered the French Huguenots in the name of the Spanish king. Henry Flagler would not permit a painting of the late admiral in the Hotel Ponce de León on the grounds that Menéndez participated in genocide.

When he died, his remains were sent to Spain. His original casket was shipped to St. Augustine, and the city commissioners voted to have it preserved in the National Shrine of Our Lady of La Leche located on the lush grounds of the Mission Nombre de Dios. In 2010, it was transferred to the museum and dedicated on the 445th anniversary of Menéndez's landing in St. Augustine.

16TH-CENTURY PEDRO MENÉNDEZ ARTIFACT

WHAT: The Menéndez coffin at the Mission Nombre de Dios Museum

WHERE: 101 San Marco Ave.

COST: Free; donations accepted

PRO TIP: The giant steel cross, erected in 1965, marks the spot in 1565 where Spanish Admiral Pedro Menéndez de Avilés and Father Lopez held the first Catholic Mass in St. Augustine.

Top: *Pedro Menéndez's empty casket in the lobby of the Mission Nombre de Dios Museum.* Inset: *Mission Nombre de Dios Museum is the site where Pedro Menéndez landed in 1565 and claimed the site for Spain and the Catholic Church.*

During the dedication, the casket made a stop at the Great Cross and statue of Father Lopez, a Spanish priest who celebrated the first Catholic Mass in St. Augustine on September 8, 1565. The casket is a physical relic of the ruthless admiral who founded the first permanent Spanish colony in America.

The ivy-covered Shrine of La Leche on the mission grounds, where the Menéndez casket has rested for decades, honors Mary the mother of Jesus and all mothers of every religion.

OLD SPANISH QUARRIES

How did the quarries save St. Augustine?

On the island of Anastasia State Park, there is a popular half-mile hiking trail open 365 days a year called the King's Coquina Quarries. The name doesn't refer to a specific king but dubs the centuries-old quarries as royal. Spanish kings and queens wanted a defense against marauders in the city of St. Augustine. The main objective of the quarries was to provide the raw material to build a fort, which was completed in the 17th century: the Castillo de San Marcos.

That makes the old Spanish quarries very old indeed, even older than the famous fort. Coquina, a rock formed from the debris of mollusks and sand, tossed by waves, and compressed beneath the earth for thousands of years, was dug from the quarries in blocks, loaded onto barges, and shipped across Matanzas Bay to St. Augustine. The medieval Castillo de San Marcos and many of the existing homes, museums, businesses, and surrounding walls of St. Augustine are made of coquina.

Without coquina, colonial St. Augustine, which suffered devasting fires and attacks from the British, may have ceased to exist. Most cities in early Florida turned

COQUINA MINING

WHAT: A picturesque spot where coquina was quarried hundreds of years ago

WHERE: Just before the entrance for Anastasia State Park on the right, 1020 Anastasia Blvd.

COST: Free

PRO TIP: The St. Johns Historical Society believes there was once a Spanish barracks on this site, but it was destroyed by fire.

The Castillo de San Marcos, completed in 1695, required 23 years of hard labor for workers mining coquina. It is one of the few completed forts in Florida.

The Old Spanish Quarries are located within Anastasia State Park in St. Augustine.

to brick as a building material, but it was expensive to ship and often in short supply. St. Augustine, luckily, had a built-in natural resource.

The quarries are listed on the National Register of Historic Places. Just before the entrance on the right of Anastasia State Park is a trail leading to the quarry remains, a peaceful place with a park bench, a walkway, shady trees, and marauding gopher tortoises who may like a nibble of lettuce from your picnic basket.

CITY GATE

What are the round stone orbs topping the city gate?

The Old City Gate is just a set of historic coquina pillars at the junction of Orange and St. George Streets. The gate is gone, but the pillars once were part of a protective wall that surrounded the city. Since Florida is a peninsula, attackers approached on land from the north with nefarious intent. This happened twice with British invasions and with numerous Indian attacks during the Seminole Wars.

In 1705, the Spanish built defenses across this northern boundary in the form of an earthen wall known as the Cubo Line, which consisted of a log barrier and dry moat. By 1808, the city gate was part of the Cubo Line and was guarded day and night.

The City Gate opens onto St. George Street.

The actual gate is gone, but portions of the original hinges are still visible on one of the pillars. Portions of the Cubo Line and other defensive barrier lines have been partially reconstructed.

Today, the City Gate consists solely of two square coquina pylons topped with stone pomegranates. They are 20 feet tall, 12 feet apart, and four feet thick. They mark the entrance to St. George Street, the busiest tourist thoroughfare in the city. Along with the Castillo de San Marcos, it is a designated item on the National Register of Historic Places and a property of the National Park Services.

THE CUBO LINE OF DEFENSE

WHAT: Iconic coquina city "Gate"

WHERE: 11 St. George St.

COST: Free

PRO TIP: The City Gate is where the 19th-century spirit of a young yellow-fever victim, Elizabeth, supposedly waves to motorists at midnight.

In 1808, the Cubo Line was six feet tall with a wide moat.

PLAZA DE LA CONSTITUCIÓN

What is unique about the design of the plaza?

On a beautiful Florida afternoon, tourists and locals convene, take pictures, and stroll among the statues and memorials of the Plaza de la Constitución. These works of art include homage to the past: to American Revolutionary War prisoners; soldiers killed in World War II, the Korean War, and the Vietnam War; the civil rights movement; and the Constitution Monument (which the plaza is named after).

However, the plaza itself is older than any statues or obelisks. It is older than the Castillo de San Marcos. Like much of St. Augustine, the plaza was established in the 16th century and adhered to the Spanish Royal Ordinances, which applied to everything in the city (even the layout of the Catholic cemetery). This is why the plaza looks a lot like a European courtyard.

The ordinances were a set of rules laid out by King Phillip II to ensure Spanish towns, cities, and colonies all looked the same. The plaza must have a rectangular shape, a cathedral, a government house, and merchants' quarters built at specific points of a compass. The Old Public Market was another requirement of the ordinance, so colonists could sell and buy wares.

In more recent eras, Florida's official state play, *Cross and Sword*, performed in the Plaza de la Constitución for 30 consecutive years. Written in 1965, the play portrays St. Augustine's history and was designed to celebrate the 400th anniversary of the former Spanish colony. In the 1960s, dance instructor and wife of then Mayor James Lindsley, Lillian Lindsley, taught local children how to perform

---

Established in 1573 by Admiral Pedro Menéndez, the Plaza de la Constitución is the oldest public place in America.

8

The Plaza de la Constitución is a rectangular park and a National Historic Landmark designed according to Spanish Royal Decree in the 16th century.

during the celebration. *Cross and Sword* performances waned in the late '90s because of a lack of funding. Today, the Plaza features concerts and a beautiful, illuminated display during the Nights of Lights festival over the winter holiday.

The Plaza de la Constitución is on the National Register of Historic Places.

THE HEART OF ST. AUGUSTINE

WHAT: A Spanish courtyard

WHERE: 1 Cathedral Pl., bordered by St. George Street, King Street, and Cathedral Place

COST: Free

PRO TIP: You can reserve the plaza gazebo for private events by contacting the City of St. Augustine.

HISTORIC PUBLIC MARKET AT THE PLAZA DE LA CONSTITUCIÓN

What is the shameful secret of the open pavilion in the Plaza de la Constitución?

The Old Public Market sits on the east end of the Plaza de la Constitución, a site of picnics and photo ops in the 21st century. Yet, its history is unsettling. The Spanish brought slaves to St. Augustine as early as the 16th century, and although the open-air pavilion was meant to sell foods and commercial goods, humans also were bought and sold there. It was historically called the Old Slave Market, and though that name attracts tourists, most locals are reluctant to use that reference.

Plaque identifying the spot where human beings were sold into slavery

For years there was debate as to whether the Historic Public Market sold enslaved Africans in St. Augustine. However, historic proof was uncovered in the 1836 version of the *St. Johns County Deed Book*, which recorded the sale of two adolescent girls. Human trafficking was not confined to the open pavilion in the northeast corner of the Plaza de la Constitución. Ralph Waldo Emerson witnessed motherless

In 2011, *St. Augustine's "Slave Market": A Visual History* by Holly Goldstein of the Savannah College of Art and Design was published in the Southern Spaces series "Landscapes and Ecologies of the US South."

The Old Public Market, also known as the Old Slave Market, is an historic open-air market building.

children auctioned off in the yard of the governor's mansion.

In the '60s, the old pavilion animated civil rights activists who mounted it to demand racial equality. Today, it serves as a backdrop for the plaza's first civil rights statute: the *St. Augustine Foot Soldiers Monument*. In his dedication speech, St. Augustine Mayor Joseph Boles Jr. said that visitors "see this monument next to the Old Slave Market where evil held forth . . . and they will know that this blessed event is designed to exorcise that nightmare."

The St. Augustine Foot Soldiers Monument depicts generic civil rights participants, instead of specific individuals, to portray a sense of community.

AN OPEN PAVILION IN THE PLAZA

WHAT: A place where human beings, vegetables, and meat were sold in an open market

WHERE: In an open-air pavilion on the east end of the plaza

COST: Free

PRO TIP: Concerts in the Plaza are held June through August at the Plaza de la Constitución.

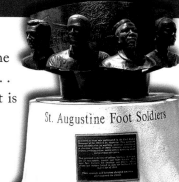

ST. GEORGE STREET

Why is the main street in St. Augustine named after an American enemy?

St. George Street in St. Augustine began, as most Florida streets did, as a dusty dirt road. Although there is no archaeological evidence that St. George Street was ever an Indian trail, according to Charles Tingley, senior research librarian of the St. Augustine Historical Society, it is possible, since:

> "St. George Street is on the crest of the ridge between the Matanzas River and Maria Sanchez Creek, and Indian trails are often on ridges between watersheds."

Forward hundreds of years, and St. George Street was paved with a variety of materials before landing on asphalt as early as 1876. Yet it is not the implementation of paving materials that defines its history. In a heavily Spanish-influenced culture, St. Augustine's main street is named after a British monarch, the mad King George III, whom American patriots fought against in 1776. One must conclude that the street naming occurred during the time of the British occupation of St. Augustine.

Today the narrow thoroughfare is blocked from traffic. Beginning at the City Gate, St. George Street is packed with tourists, couples, and families lining up for the museums, high-profile shops, restaurants, eateries, historic houses, restored houses, and replicas. The size of the crowds on the narrow street sometimes seem to rival the squeeze that hordes of Disney World tourists put on pedestrian navigation.

There's a lot worth seeing at this historic venue. Several national landmarks reside on St. George Street, such as the Oldest Wooden

---

King George III, for whom St. Augustine's main street is named, died at Windsor Castle in 1820, mad, feeble, and blind.

St. George Street is a busy pedestrian-only street in the center of the St. Augustine historic district.

School House, the Cathedral Basilica, the Ribera House, the Horruytiner/Lindsley House, the Governor's House Cultural Center & Museum, the Saint Photios Greek Orthodox National Shrine, and the Peña-Peck House Museum.

St. George Street is just as busy at night with ghost tours, scavenger hunts, and live music. Weekdays are the least crowded days to visit, especially in the morning.

THE MAIN ARTERY OF THE HISTORIC DISTRICT

WHAT: The historic and tourist center of St. Augustine

WHERE: St. George Street

COST: Free

PRO TIP: Use the Historic Downtown Parking Facility on 10 Cordova ($15) to avoid driving around pointlessly. If it's full, try a side street off Ponce de León Boulevard.

OLD SPANISH WELL AND CHIMNEY

Who stayed in these ruins during the 17th century?

Most people relegate historic ruins to European countries, but for the Indiana Jones minded, there are Spanish colonial ruins right off St. Augustine Beach.

A crumbling chimney and well are the remains of a Spanish barracks or fortress on this site. It housed the masons, stonecutters, and "workers," including Indians and slaves who sheltered or camped in this remote spot to quarry coquina (the quarry is across the street). Spanish soldiers presumably stayed there as well as overseers. The coquina was dug out of the earth, shaped into blocks, loaded on a tram or wagon, and shipped by barge or canoe across the Matanzas River to the mainland. There, the large stones were used to build the Castillo de San Marcos.

A weathered and blackened ruin of a smokestack still stands

RUINS IN ST. AUGUSTINE

WHAT: 17th-century remains of a Spanish barracks

WHERE: 1744 Old Beach Rd., St. Augustine Beach

COST: Free

PRO TIP: Coquina blocks were a popular building material for residences during the city's first Spanish rule.

Coquina are small bivalve mollusks with a tiny, smooth shell. As a rock, coquina is composed of the debris of these fossils. You can find it along the northeast coast of Florida. It is known as the "rock that saved St. Augustine" because of its ability to withstand fire and absorb the shock of cannonballs.

Left: *The Old Spanish Chimney and Well in St. Augustine are historical landmarks commemorated by the St. Johns County Historical Commission.* Right: *These ruins are believed to be part of a Spanish barracks that housed the quarry overseer and others building the Castillo de San Marcos.*

forlornly in this remote outpost, surrounded by a wooden fence with posted warnings not to "sit, stand, climb, touch, or remove coquina." Tree roots thread through the former hearth. Under a canopy to the right are the remains of the well, its design and girth a familiar sight among the older houses in the historic district.

The Old Spanish Chimney and Well are designated Historic Landmarks by the St. Johns County Historical Commission.

MAYPORT

Why is a town in Duval County included in a book about secrets of St. Augustine's St. Johns County?

Mayport is located at the mouth of the St. Johns River about 25 miles east of Jacksonville. Why is it included in a book about secrets of the ancient city of St. Augustine?

Mayport was a French colony briefly, and its history involves a lot of the same historical figures who fought, settled, and died in St. Augustine. French Admiral Jean Ribaut sailed into the St. Johns River and proclaimed Mayport for France. Although St. Augustine is the oldest continuously occupied settlement in America, Mayport was founded in 1562, three years earlier. The Mayport community came under Spanish control by 1565 when Admiral Pedro Menéndez murdered all the French settlers. He set up a military outpost at the site where the Mayport Naval Station and lighthouse exists today.

Today, Mayport is known for its role as a naval force with local and international branches. The US 4th Fleet stationed in Mayport is the third largest in the world, and its ships can be deployed internationally.

The St. Johns River Ferry, also known as the Mayport Ferry, is an automobile ferry that connects Mayport and Fort George Island, two areas within Jacksonville.

View of cruise ship on the St. Johns near Fort Caroline

FERRY TO MAYPORT

WHAT: A community older than St. Augustine available by ferry from the north

WHERE: 414 Massey Ave., Jacksonville

COST: $16 to tow a car on the ferry

PRO TIP: There is a public road to Mayport on State Road A1A.

Mayport is also known for its excellent shrimp and beautiful shrimp boats. Two popular restaurants offering fresh shrimp and seafood exist side by side in the small community. The Sand Dollar Restaurant and Singleton's Seafood Shack both offer a view of the St. Johns River, the silhouette of a shrimp boat at sunset, and, occasionally, a cruise ship on its way to Jaxport, the Jacksonville Port Authority.

The late owner of Mayport's Singleton's Seafood Shack, Captain Singleton, a man of Minorcan descent, built more than 100 wooden model boats to scale from memory. The boats are on display in the family-run restaurant.

FORT MOSE HISTORIC STATE PARK

Who was the leader and the hero of Fort Mose?

Fort Mose is a salt marsh, nature trail, and museum today, but in 1738, it was the first free Black settlement in what would someday become the United States. It originated in 1693 when the king of Spain, Charles III, declared that any escaped slave who made it to Fort Mose would be granted freedom if he converted to Catholicism and served in the Spanish militia. Indian guides helped African Americans find the fort.

The site was an important strategic spot for the Spanish to rebuff the British. The people who lived in Fort Mose came to America skilled in farming, carpentry, blacksmithing, tanning, and cobbling. Of particular note is Captain Francisco Menéndez, who was kidnapped from West Africa and enslaved by the British in South Carolina. He escaped to Spanish Florida in 1715 and fought bravely against the British, coming out the winner in several attacks. He was appointed to command Fort Mose in 1738 by Spanish Governor Montiano of Florida.

The fort was burned, rebuilt, and occupied until 1763 when the Spanish flag was exchanged for the British. The institution of slavery under British rule was considerably harsher than the Spaniard's version. All former slaves of Fort Mose and St. Augustine lost their freedom—forever. Under the English monarch's thumb, slaves could not earn and accumulate money to buy their own or family members' release from bondage. Consequently, most of the Fort Mose community immigrated to Cuba with the Spaniards, formed a new community, and stayed there.

A handmade St. Christopher medal was among the artifacts found at Fort Mose in the 1980s.

Left: *Fort Mose Historic State Park.* Right: *Walkway to the salt marshes and wildlife of Fort Mose.*

Forgotten by history, the pioneering site was revived by archaeologists in the mid-1980s and authorized as a National Historic Landmark by the federal government a decade later. The museum is open every day from 9 a.m. to 6 p.m.

SITE OF A FAMOUS FORT

WHAT: The first free Black community in the US

WHERE: 15 Fort Mose Trl.

COST: Donations accepted

PRO TIP: Reenactors stage the Battle of Bloody Mose when Captain Francisco Menéndez led Fort Mose in establishing an important war victory over Georgia governor and British General James Oglethorpe in 1740.

SPANISH MILITARY HOSPITAL MUSEUM

What ghastly discovery materialized near the front door of the museum?

The Spanish Military Hospital Museum is an historic replica of a building in St. Augustine on a street once named Hospital. The building became the first hospital in colonial St. Augustine, named Our Royal Hospital of Our Lady Guadalupe. Today it is owned by the State of Florida and managed by the University of Florida. It is a small building, less than 1,700 square feet, containing only four rooms: the ward, the morgue (also known as the mourning room), administration (once known as the surgeon's room), and the apothecary. Only Spanish soldiers were treated there, and they had to be sick, wounded, or dying, which explains the plethora of haunted tales about the old hospital that persist to this day.

The original hospital building lasted from the 1700s to 1821, but the city tore it down for new water lines. In 1966, it was restored on its original foundation with the same

ST. AUGUSTINE'S FIRST HOSPITAL

WHAT: A Spanish hospital with origins that date back to the first Spanish occupation

WHERE: 3 Aviles St.

COST: $9.50 for adults, $4.50 for children ages 5–12

PRO TIP: In the 1970s during the repair of a water line, the city discovered hundreds of skeletons and remains outside the door of the museum. The mass grave was covered up, and visitors walk over it to enter the museum.

During the British occupation of St. Augustine, the hospital was a private dwelling owned by a Scotsman named William Watson who built and renovated homes in St. Augustine.

rooms as the original hospital and resurrected as a museum. Today the street it's on is called Aviles, and it is the oldest street in the continental United States.

The old hospital offers educational tours on demand during the day, tailor-made for history buffs interested in how medicine was practiced in colonial St. Augustine. The medical museum on the second floor displays medicinal methods of the colonial Spanish occupations.

The museum is open seven days a week from 9 a.m. to 5 p.m. except on Christmas and Thanksgiving.

Exterior of the Spanish Military Hospital on Aviles Street in St. Augustine

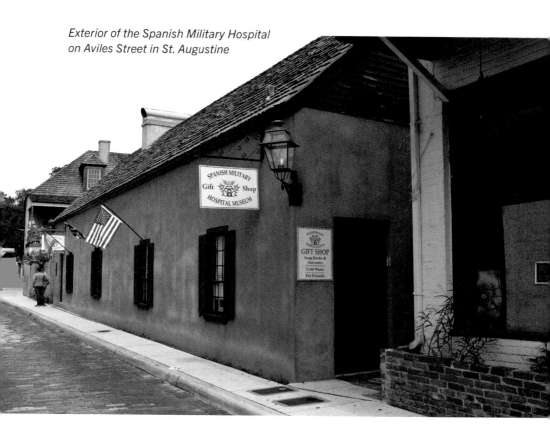

FOURTH OF JULY AT CASTILLO DE SAN MARCOS

What Revolutionary War hero was imprisoned in the medieval fort?

In 1780, soon after one of America's first Fourth of July holidays, Brig. Gen. Christopher Gadsen, the leader of the South Carolina Patriot Movement in the Revolutionary War and lieutenant governor of Charleston, was imprisoned in the Castillo.

It came about after he surrendered the city of Charleston to the British general Henry Clinton. Gadsen was confined to his home in Charleston on house arrest. Clinton was replaced by Gen. Charles Cornwallis who decided in 1780 to arrest 20 of the rebel civil officers who were on parole. They were unceremoniously rushed to a ship and taken to St. Augustine.

When they arrived, the St. Augustine governor offered them freedom on condition of what today constitutes bail. Most accepted, but Gadsen refused, claiming that the British had already breached one parole and he viewed the second as extortion. As a result, he spent the next 10 months in solitary confinement in a prison room at the old Spanish fortress, where his health deteriorated. A plaque erected in the Plaza de la Constitución by Florida's Daughters of

REVOLUTIONARY WAR HEROS WERE CONFINED HERE

WHAT: Brig. Gen. Christopher Gadsen sassed Gen. Cornwallis in 1780 and spent almost five months in solitary confinement in the Castillo de San Marcos.

WHERE: 1 Castillo Dr.

COST: $15 for adults

PRO TIP: The fort also housed the famous Seminole Indian Chief Osceola before he was transferred to Fort Moultrie in South Carolina.

Fourth of July at the Castillo de San Marcos where Gadsen was held by Cornwallis during the Revolutionary War 250 years ago

the American Revolution memorializes American prisoners of war captured by British troops and held during the American Revolution at Fort Marion (the name for the Castillo de San Marcos during the British period of occupation).

Today, the Fourth of July is a big event at the old fort with tourists and locals picnicking on the grounds designed to hold off Indians and the British.

The Gadsden Purchase of Arizona was named for Christopher Gadsen's grandson James Gadsen.

COLONIAL OAK MUSIC PARK

What centuries-old denizen inhabits the Colonial Oak Music Park?

You can tell a city has a young business forum when there is free music right in the middle of an historic downtown. Colonial Oak Music Park opened in 2015 as part of the Colonial Quarter, an interactive outdoor history museum staging the Spanish, British, and American periods of the St. Augustine colony. Patrons congregate on picnic benches under a huge oak tree, which has stood in the same spot for over five centuries.

Music park employees like to speculate how many Spanish-owned horses watered the tree. On the grounds is the St. Augustine Seafood Company, which is rumored to once have served as a horse stable. Now a restaurant offering counter and takeout service, the brand embraces "honoring and supporting the rich fishing heritage of our Nation's oldest port."

For a memorable night in downtown St. Augustine, there

NAMED AFTER AN OAK TREE FROM THE SPANISH OCCUPATION

WHAT: Free live music and entertainment in the historic downtown district

WHERE: 33 St. George St.

COST: Free

PRO TIP: Formerly a parking lot for the Colonial Spanish Quarter Living History Museum, the land is leased to Pat Croce, an NBA executive who developed the Colonial Quarter.

Some of the better-known bands who played Colonial Oak Music Park are the Mountain Goats, the Black Lillies, the Jess Zimmerman Band, and Big Engine.

Massive ancient oak tree at Colonial Oak Music Park

is nothing like modern music in an ancient setting. This place has everything. Local people and tourists visit the music park because of the variety of entertainment like open-mic nights, comedy nights, and improv shows. It's also on the festival circuit, including the Sing Out Loud Festival and the Gamble Rogers Folk Festival.

You should check it out at least once.

HUGUENOT CEMETERY

What original and unique art form is found in the public cemetery?

The Huguenot Cemetery, also known as the St. Augustine Public Burying Ground, was created to bury non-Catholics who succumbed to yellow fever, typhus, or some other deadly mishap. The cemetery was founded in 1821, the year the US acquired the territory from the Spanish, which was the year of a yellow fever epidemic, despite St. Augustine's reputation as a haven of health. It is estimated almost 200 people died. In the 19th century, it cost $4 to buy a plot, worth about $110 in 2024.

Half an acre was a working cemetery from 1821 to 1884, but it fell into disarray for many years. It's confirmed that its actual terrain and plots extend far beyond the cemetery's gates. It buried many corpses under wooden crosses, which did not last.

One-of-a-kind coquina cross at the Huguenot Cemetery

The Old Protestant Burial Ground on Castillo Drive across from the City Gate

UNIQUE FUNERARY ART

WHAT: Coquina crosses at the Huguenot Cemetery

WHERE: 10 S Castillo Dr.

COST: Free

PRO TIP: The Friends of the Huguenot Cemetery open it to the public on the third Saturday of each month from 11 a.m. to 2 p.m. Donations are accepted.

Within the gates in the middle of the cemetery stand two four-feet-high upright coquina crosses, a unique piece of funerary art not seen in perhaps any other part of the world. Because of its crumbly texture, coquina is usually shaped into blocks and used for masonry, as it was for the Castillo de San Marcos, the City Gate, and many homes. But an unknown artisan managed to shape both crosses from one very large coquina stone quarried from Anastasia Island.

Facing the crosses from A1A, the one on the right is a replica, made after the original succumbed to Hurricane Irma. But the one on the left is original albeit a bit worn and cracked.

The crosses represent the Hinckleys who died within a month of each other in 1877. The crosses are supported by coquina footstones.

Originally, non-Catholics in Spanish St. Augustine were interred near what is now SR 312 and the fishing pier.

GOVERNOR'S HOUSE CULTURAL CENTER AND MUSEUM

**What famous American hero was a guest
at the Governor's House in the 18th century?**

Known as *Casa del gobierno* in the native tongue of St. Augustine's Spanish founders, the original Government House was established in the late 16th century. The coquina building was rebuilt in the 18th century and hosted its share of famous visitors. Frontiersman Daniel Boone stopped by on a trip during St. Augustine's British period to ask permission to buy land from Governor Grant. Spanish royals visited twice in the past two decades. There is a plaque under the east balcony memorializing King Juan Carlos and Queen Sofía of Spain who made a public appearance from the east balcony in 2001. Spanish monarchs King Felipe VI and Queen Letizia visited the Governor's House in 2015.

The grand building belonged to the Spanish government, the British government, the US, and Florida's Historic Preservation Society. Now it's owned by the University of Florida, which owns other properties in St. Augustine for historic and preservation purposes. The lobby displays images and a timeline of the building's long history. A university research library occupies the second floor.

There are traveling museum exhibitions open for viewing on the ground floor that change every three to five years. Years ago, an exhibit featured an ancient Timucuan canoe and artifacts of Indian culture. Then the Spanish colonial influence was explored. In 2022, the museum featured oil paintings from the university's the *Florida*

Architect Robert Mills drew the plans for the Government House restoration in 1834. Later, he designed the *Washington Monument*.

The Governor's House Cultural Center and Museum on King Street

Art Collection, an exhibit from the Vickers family housed in the Harn Museum of Art. Titled *Painting St. Augustine*, the selection featured mostly local skylines, seascapes, and side streets from a variety of Gilded Age artists who stayed in the Ponce de León and hawked their work to the wealthy patrons who wintered in the luxurious hotel.

Exhibit hours are 10 a.m. to 5 p.m. Wednesday through Sunday.

HISTORIC GOVERNMENT BUILDING

WHAT: Famous American and European visitors have frequented the Government House since the 18th century.

WHERE: 48 King St.

COST: Free

PRO TIP: The Government House has been listed in the National Register of Historic Places since 2014.

CONSTITUTION OBELISK IN THE PLAZA DE LA CONSTITUCIÓN

What mysterious symbol was carved on the Constitution Monument?

In the early 19th century, St. Augustine was a Spanish town, which, like all Spanish towns in 1812, built its duly named Plaza de la Constitución and Constitution Monument, honoring Spain's first Royal Decree. The French Revolution was in full swing, and free thinking swept over Europe, even in Catholic Spain. It took St. Augustine Governors Alvarez and Gomez several weeks to raise the money for the monument honoring the new Spanish government.

The inlaid tablet on the monument displayed the Spanish Constitution of 1812, a progressive document at any point in time. It guaranteed federal independence, a free press, free trade, and a limited monarchy with the division of government entities.

Two years later, politics swung the other way, and the Spanish government was returned to King

REMNANT FROM THE FIRST SPANISH OCCUPATION

WHAT: A monument that is the only one of its kind left in the world

WHERE: In the Plaza de la Constitución at 1 Cathedral Pl.

COST: Free

PRO TIP: Spain's Royal Decree was like America's Declaration of Independence, forming a constitutional governing body rather than a monarchy. In Spain, it did not last.

A Masonic symbol mysteriously appeared on the constitution tablet during one of its removals. No one knows when it was carved or who did it.

The mysterious Mason symbol, featured on the bottom, was not on the original plaque.

Constitution Obelisk in the Plaza de la Constitución.

Ferdinand VII. All the constitutional monuments in Spain and in the colonies were marked for destruction. St. Augustine, considered the capital province of east Spain's colonized territory, did not comply. The obelisk-shaped monument was retained as a symbol of Spain's liberal constitution and the governance of the past. It is the only remaining monument of its kind in the world.

Made of stone and coquina, it is the plaza's oldest monument and, at 30 feet, the tallest. It is a National Historic Landmark.

CANNON FIRE IN ST. AUGUSTINE

When and where do cannons fire in St. Augustine?

Dominating the St. Augustine landscape is the Castillo de San Marcos, a medieval-style fort ordered into being in 1672 after the city got tired of British raids burning down the town. From all accounts, the Spanish conquistadors were averse to manual labor, so for the next 23 years, slaves, freemen, and Indians labored to build the giant structure. Made from coquina, an indigenous kind of rock mined from Anastasia Island, the Castillo is one of the few completed forts in Florida—and the oldest. It was part of the Cubo Line along with the City Gate, protecting the city from invaders from the north. That's where the cannons came in.

WEEKEND DISPLAYS

WHAT: Cannon fire in St. Augustine

WHERE: 11 S Castillo Dr.

COST: Exhibition is free.

PRO TIP: The Castillo de San Marcos is a National Historic Monument.

The cannons were important in repelling invaders such as the Indians and Brits. In more modern times, such as the 1960s, cannons shook the city at 6 p.m. every day. People marked the time, even solved crimes, based on the precision of the explosion. Today, there are three dozen authentic old cannons scattered about the gun deck of the Castillo, but they are not used during weekend demonstrations with cannon reenactors. Instead, three replica iron cannons on the

The Fountain of Youth also sets off cannons on the weekend.

Colonial reenactors fire cannons from the Castillo de San Marcos.

northeast gun deck are fired weekly, usually on Friday, Saturday, and Sunday. You can hear them at 10:30 a.m., 11:30 a.m., 1:30 p.m., 2:30 p.m., and 3:30 p.m.

AVENIDA MENÉNDEZ SEAWALL

What 19th-century West Point cadet was court-martialed for incompetence in reconstructing the St. Augustine seawall?

The St. Augustine seawall, an historic walkway, shields the city of St. Augustine from inundating waters caused by the Matanzas Bay and, by extension, the Atlantic Ocean. Keeping rising seawater out of the city was always a struggle. Erected by the Spanish around the end of the 17th century, the seawall has been restored, and even reconstructed, more than once.

When Spain ceded Florida to the US, part of the seawall was plundered by the US military to construct lodging for soldiers. The Florida National Guard Headquarters on Marine Street behind O. C. White's Seafood & Spirits was constructed from the raided seawall. Over 300 years old, it's called St. Francis Barracks. But breaking up the seawall caused the waterfront and surrounding property to flood. The government hired West Point graduates to repair the damage.

The 19th-century officer in charge of designing a new seawall and supervising its construction was court-martialed for doing an inexpert job and for wasting the allocated money. His name is on the St. Augustine Sea Wall kiosk on San Marco Avenue as one of the engineers: Lt. Stephen Tuttle (1797–1835, class of 1820).

Over the years, devastation from its age, tides, squalls, and hurricanes required extensive repairs to the old wall. FEMA contributed millions to ensure the historic seawall and encompassing

---

Walking alongside the seawall and observing the moon on Matanzas Bay has served as a romantic stroll over the centuries.

View of Avenida Menéndez Seawall from Matanzas Bay

harbor area were protected. Made of coquina reinforced with concrete and steel, the seawall is capped with stone rimming America's oldest harbor. Originally it only covered the area south from the Castillo de San Marcos to the Plaza de la Constitución. Today, it is four feet wide, about one mile long, and spans the Castillo de San Marcos to the government barracks.

ERECTED BY WEST POINT CADETS

WHAT: Coquina wall protecting property on the waterfront

WHERE: 135 Avenida Menéndez

COST: Free

PRO TIP: In centuries past, the waters of Matanzas Bay used to extend as far as the edge of the Historic Public Market.

FOUNTAIN OF YOUTH ARCHAEOLOGICAL PARK

Did Ponce de León really land in St. Augustine in 1513?

The Fountain of Youth is a tourist attraction, but it was the land of Timucua Indians for 3,000 years. In the 16th century, it was the first Spanish settlement in St. Augustine. Validated by the Smithsonian Institute in an archaeological dig, the 15-acre historical tourist attraction is much more than a well of sulfur water that was believed to magically prolong youth.

The origin of the 1513 myth concerns the former governor of Puerto Rico, Ponce de León. The explorer, allegedly searching for the Fountain of Youth, probably first came ashore farther south in Melbourne, Florida. Mentions of the Fountain of Youth do not appear in his writings. It is likely that if Ponce de León did show up in St. Augustine, it was to find potable drinking water for his crew.

There was another Spaniard who walked these grounds in 1565; Admiral Pedro Menéndez established the first continuously occupied colony on land that became the United States. There is a statue of the conquistador commemorating the site where the settlement was founded. Throughout the park there are native and Spanish artifacts, a watchtower, reenactors of 16th-century trades, and a reconstruction of the original mission church from 1587.

Previous owners of the property include a British florist named Henry Williams who purchased the grounds in 1868 and named it Paradise Grove. Williams hired two men to dig a well on his property, and that well became what is known as the Fountain of Youth.

Like the Castillo de San Marcos, the cannon at the archaeological settlement is fired several times a day, usually on weekends.

Top: *Fountain of Youth Archaeological Park's coquina cross marker.* Inset: *The Coquina Cross*

A FAMOUS WELL

WHAT: Site of the original settlement of St. Augustine

WHERE: 11 Magnolia Ave.

COST: $17.11 for adults, $8.40 for children ages 6–12

PRO TIP: The well dug in the 19th century still spouts sulfur water for tourists to drink, though with no discernable effects on their age. It is encased in a spring house made of coquina in the mission revival style.

Later the place was purchased by a flamboyant physician and gold prospector named Diamond Lil. She discovered the 16th-century coquina cross on the grounds, which points to the well. Declaring it was placed by Ponce de León, she began charging admission for sightseers. The last owner, Walter Fraser, who purchased the spot in 1927, expanded the property as a tourist site.

FORT MATANZAS NATIONAL PARK

What Florida governor, later an American president, neglected this fort to the point of deterioration?

The Fort Matanzas National Park is also the site of the infamous 1565 massacre conducted by the Spanish Admiral Pedro Menéndez against Jean Ribaut and his French soldiers at the Matanzas Inlet. A marker signals the approximate spot where it occurred. Matanzas means "slaughter" in Spanish.

The history of the fort is less gory. Built in 1742 during the first Spanish period, Fort Matanzas is another coquina fort, this one installed on a barrier island named Rattlesnake. Since the Matanzas River flows beside the island, the fort was built to guard the inlet after a lengthy British siege in 1740. It was intended as a backup to the Castillo de San Marcos, 14 miles south. Aside from the fort, the park comprises about 100 acres of salt marsh along the Matanzas River.

Fast-forward to the 1820s, and the coquina fort was a ruin and uninhabitable. It cost a lot of money to maintain and to restore a federal outpost. Governor Andrew Jackson tried to sell the stone fort, but there was no interest in restoration. Barrier islands don't stay in one place because of waves that move the sand. The walls of the fort began to crack. Jackson let the fort continue to deteriorate until it was literally dropping into the ocean.

In the early 20th century, the United States Department of War undertook restoration. Walls were fixed, and the foundation evened out. Renovations, rebuilding, and repairs continue today.

Marker indicating the spot where Ribault and his men were killed by Spanish soldiers

Fort Matanzas National Park

The fort is a National Monument operated by the National Park Service in combination with the Castillo de San Marcos National Monument. There are reenactments of defensive battles by historians in colonial costumes.

Entrance to the park is restricted to the Fort Matanzas Passenger Ferry, which transports tourists from the visitor center dock to Rattlesnake Island. Tickets are issued at the Fort Matanzas Visitor Center within the park and are available on a first come basis. The ferry operates every hour from 9:30 a.m. to 3:30 p.m., Wednesday through Sunday.

FERRY TO THE FORT

WHAT: An historic 18th-century fort

WHERE: 8635 A1A S

COST: The ferry and entrance to the fort are free.

PRO TIP: Collectors can purchase a commemorative coin at the Fort Matanzas gift shop with the name of the fort misspelled. It should be worth a pirate fortune someday.

Visitors to St. Augustine can pick up a coin collector's book at the Fountain of Youth gift shop.

OLDEST HOUSE MUSEUM COMPLEX

How do museums reflect the concerns of a past community?

In St. Augustine, Spanish Colonial architecture dominates the look of individual homesteads; the layout of the city follows Spanish design principles down to the cemeteries. The González-Alvarez House, built in 1723, is widely believed to be the oldest house in St. Augustine with architecture representative of the first Spanish colonial occupation. Like most of the structures from the early Spanish colonial period, it displays thick coquina walls on the first floor, small windows, wooden beams, shutters, and covered wooden balconies on the second floor.

A representative property of Spanish, British, and American influences, four owners successively maintained the estate until the St. Augustine Historical Society took over. It is a designated National Historic Landmark with seasonal statues from the 1890 Chicago World's Fair contemplating the courtyard.

The González-Alvarez House is one of three structures comprising the complex, which includes two museums, a map gallery, a botanical garden, replicas of a colonial kitchen, and bedroom and living quarters spanning five centuries of history. These relics and replicas are precious, especially since the St. Augustine Historical Society Museum collections were damaged three times by fire.

John Stephensen, a docent and tour guide at the Oldest House Museum, likes to point out a rare fire hat from the 1800s Ponce de León brigade. It is the only one of its kind and a relic from a private task force housed in the Hotel Ponce de León around the

Today, docent Stephensen reports that firemen worldwide beg to borrow the only fire hat to survive the Ponce de León brigade.

Top: *González-Alvarez House at the Oldest House museum complex.*
Inset: *Oldest House Museum Complex displays rare fireman hat from the Ponce de León brigade.*

A PRICELESS RELIC FROM EARLY FIREFIGHTERS

WHAT: The only surviving fire hat from the Ponce de León brigade

WHERE: 14 St. Frances St.

COST: $12.95 with discounts for students, children, military, and seniors

PRO TIP: The Tovar House holds the collection for the St. Augustine Surf Culture & History Museum adjoining the Oldest House.

time the luxury resort opened for business. In those days, instead of one firehouse, independent brigades around town fought fires. The Hotel Ponce de León had electrical lights, which were constantly shorting out and even exploding. Given St. Augustine's propensity for fire, Flagler thought it prudent to be prepared.

OLDEST WOODEN SCHOOLHOUSE HISTORIC MUSEUM & GARDENS

Is the St. Augustine attraction really the oldest wooden schoolhouse in the US?

Located near the City Gate in what was once a Minorcan settlement, St. Augustine's oldest wooden schoolhouse is made of cypress and cedar logs that were timbered centuries ago. The shabby building claims to be the oldest wooden schoolhouse in America. Historians claim it is not. The Voorlezer's House in New York is older and still standing. However, that school is only partially made of wood because it has a concrete foundation. So, the St. Augustine schoolhouse may still have a claim on the "oldest" wooden schoolhouse designation because only wood is recorded for its construction.

According to tax records, the schoolhouse dates to colonial times when it was owned by a resident named Juan Genoply. Seeing a need to educate the Minorcan children, he created a schoolhouse setting in his home and thus became St. Augustine's first documented teacher. He taught children in the one-room schoolhouse for over three decades while he and his family lived upstairs. When he died, his two daughters continued his work.

The historical museum and gardens consists of five properties on the Old Schoolhouse grounds. These include the two-story, 18th-

Minorcans can be traced back to the Spanish island of Minorca in the Mediterranean Sea. Today, St. Augustine holds the largest number of Minorcan descendants in America.

century wooden schoolhouse, a separate kitchen, a well, an outhouse, and the garden. All the structures feature relics from the colonial period. The garden also exhibits sculptures of Hispanic educators such as José Martí, Cuban poet and revolutionary. There is also a bust of Juan Genoply, one of Florida's first educators and a leader among the Minorcan colonists.

Visitors may follow a self-guided tour that uses modern technology to animate a teacher and student when a sensor detects visitors. The schoolhouse is open from 10 a.m. to 6 p.m. every day except Christmas.

Oldest Wooden Schoolhouse Historic Museum & Gardens

A COLONIAL SCHOOLHOUSE

WHAT: A wooden schoolhouse claiming to be the oldest in the United States

WHERE: 14 St. George St.

COST: $6.95 for adults, $5.95 for students, free for children under five

PRO TIP: The old wooden schoolhouse is made entirely of wood except for a 1,400-pound chain that wraps around the building, anchoring it against hurricanes since the 1930s.

HORRUYTINER/ LINDSLEY HOUSE

What makes this old Spanish house so famous?

Made of coquina, the Horruytiner/Lindsley House at 214 St. George Street, across from the Trinity Episcopal Church, is one of the oldest houses in St. Augustine. In accordance with King Phillip II's Royal Spanish Ordinance, the house is built right up against the street buffered by thick exterior walls. On the southeast corner is the only freestanding wall made of tabby in St. Augustine. A tabby construction is made of shells like coquina, only it uses whole oyster shells instead of tiny clam husks. Tabby houses in St. Augustine otherwise have disappeared. This remaining wall is covered for protection except on the southeast end to display its tabby origin. There is a commemorative plaque nearby.

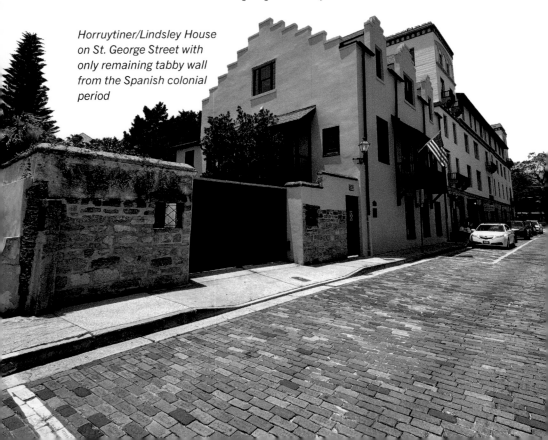

Horruytiner/Lindsley House on St. George Street with only remaining tabby wall from the Spanish colonial period

The house dates back to Don Pedro Horruytiner, the original Spanish owner of the property and governor during the first Spanish period in 1646. The house remained in his name until 1763 when the Spanish in St. Augustine emigrated to Cuba. Since then, owners of many nationalities have lived there. Among them was the Lindsley family, well known in St. Augustine. James Lindsley, a commissioner and a mayor, was involved in local politics most of his professional life.

The house is listed on the National Register of Historic Places.

AN HISTORIC CONSTRUCTION

WHAT: The only remaining freestanding tabby wall in St. Augustine

WHERE: 214 St. George St.

COST: Free

PRO TIP: James Lindsley used the house as a real estate office in the 1970s.

The house has survived storms and fires for over four centuries.

XIMENEZ-FATIO HOUSE MUSEUM

What famous writer wintered at the boardinghouse on Hospital Street?

The Ximenez-Fatio House is a white two-story mansion built of coquina. It is also 225 years old, making it one of the oldest houses in St. Augustine. It's an interesting architectural mix of the Spanish colonial style and the British influence of Federal design: a house built in a square or rectangular shape and on two or three levels.

ONE OF ST. AUGUSTINE'S OLDEST HOUSES

WHAT: A 19th-century winter resort for St. Augustine snowbirds, including a famous writer

WHERE: 20 Aviles St.

COST: $10

PRO TIP: The Ximenez-Fatio House Museum is still managed by women who sponsor art shows and book fairs on the grounds, maintain the museum and gift shop, and provide tours of the house.

Evidence of people living on the Ximenez-Fatio grounds goes back to the 16th century, but the house is named for Don Ximenez, a Spanish businessman who built it in 1798 for his Minorcan bride, Juana Pellicer. There is a history of women owning and managing the property. Louisa Fatio, the last owner, was a single woman who ran a boardinghouse previously managed by a woman. She purchased the property in 1855, owning the boardinghouse during the Civil War and Reconstruction. The house remained in her family until the 1930s.

Boardinghouses were popular places to stay in St. Augustine before the advent of Henry Flagler's hotels. Snowbirds and invalids would remain all winter. American writer Constance Fenimore Woolson stayed several winters at the Ximenez-Fatio House and wrote about it in one of her short stories, "The Ancient City." She ironically described the "hilarious

Book fair on the Ximenez-Fatio grounds

joy of the Ancient City over the coming of its annual victim, the gold-bearing Northern tourist."

Today, the museum is owned and managed by the Florida chapter of the National Society of the Colonial Dames of America. The Ximenez-Fatio House is on the National Register of Historic Places and is a designated Florida Heritage Landmark.

This house is acknowledged as the best-maintained and most genuine residence in St. Augustine from the first Spanish period.

PEÑA-PECK HOUSE MUSEUM

A HOUSE LOCATED IN THE HISTORIC DISTRICT

WHAT: A house known as the Woman's Exchange of St. Augustine

WHERE: 143 St. George St.

COST: Donations accepted

PRO TIP: The house was built for Spanish Royal Treasurer Juan Estevan de Peña during the first Spanish period and bought by Dr. Seth Peck for $918 in 1837.

Which Peña-Peck owner bequeathed her fortune to her pet?

Built of stucco, wood, and concrete in 1750 during the First Spanish Colonial Period, this is a house that reflects each era of St. Augustine occupation within a substantial 7,000 square feet. It is owned by the City of St. Augustine.

The Peña-Peck House Museum is home to the Woman's Exchange, the second-oldest organization in the ancient city. Organized in 1892, the Woman's Exchange met at the Alcazar Hotel until 1932, when the

Peña-Peck House Museum on St. George Street, formerly the Woman's Exchange

Great Depression took its toll on Flagler's hotels. It moved to the Peña-Peck House, which was left to the organization by a former member. She requested that women manage the house and give tours, which is followed to this day.

In those days, a divorce or the death of a husband could mean lifelong poverty for upper-class women sheltered from the world and discouraged from employment. The Woman's Exchange enabled women to discreetly sell jewelry, furniture, furs, and even baked goods when hard times descended. Owners' items were identified by a number, not a name, so no one was embarrassed.

Miss Anna Burt, a single millionaire and the granddaughter of one of the owners, lived in the house with her parrot, Polly, from 1912 to 1931. Apparently the two were close because Miss Burt willed Polly as her beneficiary for the remainder of its life. She also left money to Flagler Hospital and Rollins College. Then she donated the Peña-Peck House Museum to the Woman's Exchange.

During the tour, visitors may observe a pristine chamber pot under the bed, which was a standard item in St. Augustine bedrooms during the European and territorial years.

CASA MONICA RESORT & SPA

Who was Monica?

This was Flagler's third premier hotel location, which he purchased in 1889 from Franklin Smith who named it after his daughter Monica. Flagler's vision of St. Augustine was of a cultured and luxurious haven for the well-to-do. He called it the Cordova Hotel.

Made of poured concrete and designed in the style of Moorish Revival, Flagler always intended the hotel to be an extension of his other hotels. Throughout its tenure, the Cordova Hotel had a bridge that spanned to his adjacent Alcazar Hotel. During the Great Depression of the 1930s, the hotel closed and was used primarily to store furniture and boxes from Flagler's other ailing resorts. In the 1960s, it was revived as the St. Johns County courthouse, which infamously kept police dogs in the lobby to unleash on civil rights demonstrators.

FORMER FLAGLER HOTEL

WHAT: The former Cordova Hotel

WHERE: 95 Cordova St.

COST: Around $300 a night

PRO TIP: The hotel is known for its prominent display of artwork, including portraits and landscapes from local and international artists. The gallery is open to the public, and all art is for sale. The hotel participates in St. Augustine's First Friday Art Walk.

The original owner of Casa Monica, Franklin Smith, also built the Moorish Revival Villa Zorayda a few blocks away.

Casa Monica Resort & Spa, one of Flagler's three luxury hotels in the 19th century

By the late 1990s, the hotel was restored to its original beauty and regained its original name of Casa Monica. Situated in historic downtown, it's within walking distance of most of the "secrets" listed in this book. The cobblestone streets outside the glass doors of the hotel beckon tourists to take in the sights of the closest thing to a 19th-century European village in America.

The hotel is a National Historic Landmark.

PONCE DE LEÓN STATUES

What former St. Augustine mayor is responsible for the bronze Ponce de León Memorial located at the east end of Plaza de la Constitución, across from the Bridge of Lions?

There are three statues of Juan Ponce de León in St. Augustine, which is perfect irony since no one is sure if he even visited the "city" before it was colonized. One Ponce statue has ushered tourists onto the grounds of the Fountain of Youth since 1923. Another went up in 2013, located at the Guana Tolomato Matanzas National Estuarine Research Reserve in Ponte Vedra Beach. The spot replicates the natural environment of sea oats and sand closest to where historians calculate the explorer ventured onto land.

The third Ponce piece was donated by former St. Augustine mayor and Henry Flagler pal Dr. Andrew Anderson. Mounted on a 15-foot granite stand in a traffic circle fronting A1A and King Street, the likeness of the explorer is made of bronze. It is a replica of the memorial in Puerto Rico at the Plaza de San Jose in San Juan. St. Augustine's Ponce was erected 31 years after the original statue in Puerto Rico from the same mold. The Spaniard's sculpture in St. Augustine was commemorated in 1929, almost 400 years after he perished from a native's poison arrow.

The Ponce de León statue near the Bridge of Lions depicts the former governor of Puerto Rico wearing a feathered hat, body armor, and boots that reach the tops of his 16th-century-style Spanish pantaloons. He points north. The inscription reads, "The Discoverer of Florida Juan Ponce de León landed near this spot 1513." It's more likely he landed near the statue in Ponte Verda. Or

Made by C. Bupert in New York in 1888, the Puerto Rican statue of Ponce de León is made of melted steel from British cannons.

Bronze statue of Ponce de León in a traffic circle fronting A1A and King Street

in Melbourne. Or near the coquina cross at the Fountain of Youth. No one really knows.

ITALIAN ART REPLICA

WHAT: Statue of Juan Ponce de León

WHERE: 9 King St.

COST: Free

PRO TIP: Some tour guides like to say that the statue in the traffic circle is the same height as the explorer when he was alive. But there are no records of Ponce de León's height almost 500 years ago.

PYRAMIDS AT ST. AUGUSTINE NATIONAL CEMETERY

What lies under three pyramids in a quiet neighborhood cemetery?

In one of the oldest parts of the city, near the southern end of the St. Augustine National Cemetery, are three eight-foot coquina pyramids. The sloping structures are named after Major Francis Dade and his "last command," an event remembered today as the Dade Massacre. The vaults capped by the Dade Pyramids contain the remains of 1,468 US soldiers who died from 1835 to 1842. Many of these men perished in the Dade Massacre. The erection of the pyramids dates back to the end of the Seminole Wars, and they are the oldest monuments in any national cemetery.

The major and his men were wiped out by Seminole warriors during the Second Seminole War, which began on December 28, 1835. Led by their chiefs (Osceola, Jumper, Alligator, and Micanopy), the Seminoles went on the warpath because of US demands that they move to undeveloped territory.

Chief Micanopy shot Dade dead as the major passed on horseback through the pine-and-palmetto-fringed Indian trail toward neighboring Fort King. Few soldiers survived the attack. The Second Seminole War, which ended in 1842, did not have a peace treaty. Most of the Seminoles were forcibly removed to

SYMBOL OF A LAST COMMAND

WHAT: Dade Pyramids at the National Cemetery

WHERE: 104 Marine St.

COST: Free

PRO TIP: The National Cemetery is located in the National Historic Landmark district.

Three pyramids at the National Cemetery on Marine Street

Oklahoma. The US soldiers who lost their lives were at first buried on the battlefield and later disinterred to lie under the pyramids at the National Cemetery.

The National Cemetery features a 20-foot pillar known as the *Dade Monument.*

MOULTRIE CHURCH AND WILDWOOD CEMETERY

What historic church was built on the grounds of an old cemetery?

Built in 1877 on the site of Wildwood Cemetery, Moultrie Church is a white, wooden structure made of hard board and pine. Although picturesque, its doors are locked and some of the windows are boarded up. Originally Moultrie was the only Southern Methodist church in St. Johns County, but it became nondenominational until it discontinued services altogether in 2006.

It is a peaceful place, surrounded by woods and a rural community. The cemetery is older than the church, and St. Augustine pioneers dating back to the 1800s are buried there. Some of the older grave sites sit toward the back, closer to the line of trees leading into a wooded area. There are some 19th-century graves of Civil War soldiers, identified as such by the dates of their lifespans and the icon of crossed sabers. World War I veterans are buried there as well. There is at least one child's grave identifiable by its miniature size and the stone lamb perched on its headstone.

Many of the grave inscriptions are undecipherable or hand drawn on concrete. There is no doubt that all who rest there are not identified

A Civil War–era headstone at Wildwood Cemetery

The church also has been called Wildwood Church and St. Mary's by the Sea.

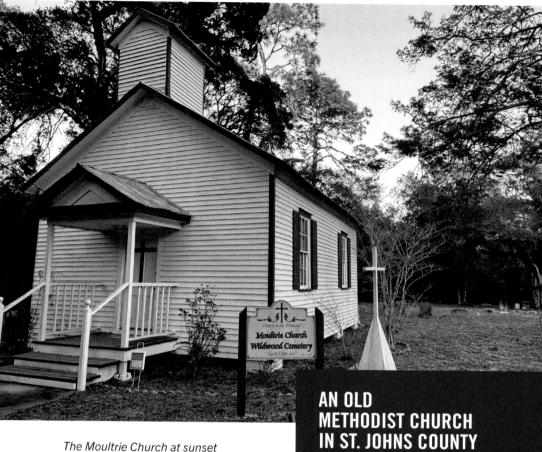

The Moultrie Church at sunset

AN OLD METHODIST CHURCH IN ST. JOHNS COUNTY

WHAT: A small church surrounded by the graves of Civil War soldiers, pioneers, and St. Augustine citizens

WHERE: 480 Wildwood Dr.

COST: Free

PRO TIP: The caretakers of the church and cemetery are Anthony Hagen, who has ancestors buried in the Wildwood Cemetery, and Chrissy Hope.

by markers as many of the old Southern cemeteries buried their dead with wooden crosses, which deteriorated. However, the historic cemetery appears to be weeded and well-tended despite its age.

Moultrie Church and Wildwood Cemetery are listed on the National Register of Historic Places.

ST. AUGUSTINE LIGHTHOUSE & MARITIME MUSEUM

What structure has been an ongoing aid to maritime navigation for 150 years?

This is not the original St. Augustine lighthouse. Built to replace a lighthouse that eventually fell into the sea from erosion, the current lighthouse is 165 feet tall and has 219 steps to the top. The lighthouse is also St. Augustine's oldest brick structure, completed in 1874. It is still an active aid to navigation because of its Fresnel lens, which includes prisms above and below the light source that redirect the light straight out to the horizon as much as 20 to 30 miles away. Credited with providing the first lighting for Florida's Atlantic coast, the Fresnel lens is named after its engineer inventor Augustin-Jean Fresnel. The nine-foot lens towered over the Paris lightkeeper who could not have guessed that 150 years later, it would still be in use as one of the few functioning lighthouses left in the United States.

A FAMOUS LANDMARK

WHAT: An efficient Fresnel lens in a functioning lighthouse

WHERE: 100 Red Cox Rd.

COST: $15 for adults, $13 for children under 12. Tours range from $20 to $40.

PRO TIP: The grounds and the lighthouse are owned by the museum as a nonprofit agency. All fees and donations directly enable the preservation of maritime and lighthouse history.

A 19th-century derelict boat recently discovered near the Bridge of Lions is protected in the St. Augustine Lighthouse & Maritime Museum.

The St. Augustine Lighthouse is visible from the historic district, creating a skyline with the treetops beyond the Bridge of Lions. The lighthouse is visible throughout any purview of Anastasia Island. Suburban neighborhoods adjoin its grounds, and children play on the swing set across the street. The lobby is filled with books by local authors about St. Augustine history, various ornaments, T-shirts, and etched glassware. It's also where tickets are sold to visit the museum and climb the lighthouse. A variety of historical and haunted tours are offered.

Working St. Augustine Lighthouse & Maritime Museum with Fresnel lens

LIGHTNER MUSEUM

Does the late owner of the Gilded Age museum patrol the grounds?

Otto Lightner was a Chicago-based publisher of a magazine about hobbies, and he bought Henry Flagler's Alcazar Hotel in 1947 to house his Gilded Age collection. He died three years after in a traumatic car crash and left the Lightner Museum to the city that griped his collection brought no revenue or taxes. Lightner's only condition for this generous gift was that the city maintain his collection in perpetuity. Perhaps his grave on the grounds was insurance on that promise.

It is a beautiful building. Henry Flagler built the Moorish-Spanish-designed Alcazar Hotel and Casino in 1888. There was a sulfur bath, a steam room, and the first indoor swimming pool in Florida at 120 feet long by 50 feet wide effused with artesian water. Today, where the deep end used to be, is Café Alcazar, an establishment with intimate tables set for lunch seven days a week from 11 a.m. to 3 p.m.

Take a turn in the beautifully landscaped courtyard or shop the

FINAL RESTING PLACE OF AN AVID COLLECTOR

WHAT: Otto Lightner's grave at the Lightner Museum

WHERE: 25 Granada St., outside the Café Alcazar and over the bridge

COST: Average of $15 to get in the museum. Café Alcazar menu ranges from $15 to $20. It's free to stroll around the grounds.

PRO TIP: In the 19th century, Henry Flagler owned the three preeminent hotels in St. Augustine: Ponce de Leon, Cordova, and Alcazar. The Ponce de León is now Flagler College, the Cordova is the Casa Monica, and the Alcazar is the Lightner Museum.

In the 19th century, a bridge connected the Alcazar and Cordova Hotels.

The Lightner Museum and Otto Lightner's final resting place

surrounding antique stores. If you cross over a small bridge, you see the large white headstone of Otto Lightner, the man who filled the museum with his collection of Gilded Age treasures. He is also the man who made the museum an erstwhile cemetery for his remains. Guests fancifully claim to see the former owner walking in the courtyard or near the front gate.

THE SUNDIAL AT FLAGLER COLLEGE

How do Flagler College students learn an ancient method of timekeeping?

Originally, the land where Henry Flagler, of Standard Oil fame, built his luxury hotel was swampy marsh. He took sand and fill from the ruins of the first free Black community in the US (Fort Mose) to construct his luxury hotel. Designed by New York architects, it was called the Ponce, short for the Hotel Ponce de León. One of the three sister hotels in St. Augustine (Ponce, Alcazar, and Cordova), it opened for business in 1888, hosting the likes of Thomas Edison, Ulysses S. Grant, and Marjorie Kinnan Rawlings. It closed its doors in 1967 following a nationwide trend favoring economically friendly roadside hotels versus swanky accommodations.

Although it was not intended to become a school, the Ponce became accredited as Flagler College in 1973. It is a beautiful, poured concrete building in the style of the Spanish Renaissance with Louis Comfort Tiffany stained glass windows in the college dining hall. There are many curious and secret facts about the building, which begin just beyond Flagler's statue and the city gate.

The centerpiece courtyard, designed like a Celtic cross, has a working sundial, compliments of the frog fountain. The center of the fountain looks like the hilt of a sword, perhaps King Arthur's Excalibur, infused with magic power. The sword's rounded knob at the top is decorated with lion heads. It is a functional fountain, surrounded by 12 terra-cotta frogs around the perimeter and four

Before the college was air-conditioned, students used to complain about the smell of sulfur coming from the fountain through their open windows.

The frog fountain at Flagler College is a working sundial.

turtles at the base of the fountain. The spitting frogs mark the hours, and the turtles mark the season. When the sun shines down on the fountain, it generates a shadow, pointing to the time of day, as it has for 135 years so far. In this picture, the time of day is 3:45 p.m.

RELIC OF A LUXURY HOTEL

WHAT: An 135-year-old sundial

WHERE: 74 King St.

COST: Free

PRO TIP: *Stolen Moments*, starring Rudolph Valentino, had scenes from the Hotel Ponce de León courtyard.

BRIDGE OF LIONS

What are the names of the lions on the famous bridge?

The Bridge of Lions is an important thruway, a functional icon, and a symbol of St. Augustine. Extending over the Matanzas Bay, it links St. Augustine with Anastasia Island. It is also a double-leaf drawbridge to accommodate tall boats.

Construction began in 1925 to replace a wooden toll bridge built in the 19th century known only as the South Beach railroad bridge. Considered decrepit by locals, the wooden bridge was weakened because of the influx of automobiles and the accommodation of a trolley, which debilitated the bridge to and from the ancient city.

Dr. Andrew Anderson, a mayor, friend of Henry Flagler, and a footnote in numerous volumes of St. Augustine history, donated two marble lions copied from statues in Italy. They were named Firm and Faithful and serve as sentries at the foot of the west end of the bridge. On the east side of the bridge on Anastasia Island are a pair of granite lions named Peace and Happiness. The bridge underwent

The Bridge of Lions features marble lions Firm and Faithful.

another restoration in the 21st century.

The Bridge of Lions has sidewalks on its perimeter for strolling and is listed on the National Register of Historic Places. Walking it is just under a mile round trip and constitutes a pleasant way to view St. Augustine sights, such as the Castillo de San Marcos setting off cannons, *Schooner Freedom* gracefully cutting a path along the intercoastal waterway, and sun boats and sailboats dotting Matanzas Bay.

A LINK BETWEEN TWO ISLANDS

WHAT: Bookmarking the bridge are a quartet of famous lion sculptures copied from Italian masters in Florence.

WHERE: 20 Bridge of Lions

COST: Free

PRO TIP: During the Nights of Lights festival in December and January, you can see the downtown historic district light up from the top of the bridge.

If you want to make a night of it, a good nearby dinner spot is Amici Italian Restaurant on A1A. You can watch the Nights of Lights on video cam there and avoid the crowds.

FLAGLER MEMORIAL PRESBYTERIAN CHURCH

What St. Augustine founding father rests in eternal peace in an adjoining mausoleum?

Rev. Dr. Camp, the pastor of Flagler Memorial Presbyterian Church and a Flagler college grad, is so cool he wrote a book about surfing. Like most of the population of the St. Augustine business district, he is young and well-educated, living and working in a famous city known for being ancient. He and his wife, who is also a minister, lead a church donated by its singular founder, and its history is somewhat dominated by him as well.

Flagler Memorial Presbyterian Church is yet another building constructed by Henry Flagler. In this case, he wanted to honor the memory of his adult daughter, Jennie Louise, in the faith of her grandfather, a Presbyterian minister. She rests in eternal peace in a marble mausoleum on the grounds, along with most of the Flagler family.

FIRST PRESBYTERIAN CHURCH IN SPANISH ST. AUGUSTINE

WHAT: Flagler family mausoleum and founding Presbyterian church

WHERE: 32 Sevilla St.

COST: Donations accepted

PRO TIP: The church represents the first significant Protestant church in an historically Catholic city.

Flagler Memorial Presbyterian Church is one of the largest and oldest poured concrete buildings in the United States.

The church was the first Presbyterian congregation in Florida. In 1824, worship began in members' homes, which was the custom for the times. Then there was a Presbyterian church on St. George Street, which eventually flourished into the stunning Venetian Renaissance–style cathedral with the gold detail and copper dome on Sevilla Street. It was Flagler's gift to his adopted city.

Cited as one of the top eight Religious Wonders of the World by CNN, the interior contains imported Italian marble floors, a one-piece marble baptismal font, stained glass windows, and pews made of mahogany. There are services on Sunday at 8:30 and 11:00 a.m.

Henry Flagler and relatives rest in peace at Flagler Memorial Presbyterian Church.

ZORA NEALE HURSTON HOUSE

Will the old boardinghouse become a museum or fodder for the bulldozer?

Writer and anthropologist Zora Neale Hurston was a wayfaring vagabond and merry prankster a generation before the likes of Jack Kerouac and Ken Kesey made it cool. She also was a contemporary and colleague of prominent Florida folklorist Stetson Kennedy. She never really settled down, living at friends' houses, on houseboats, and even in Haiti for a spell.

Along with Stetson Kennedy, Hurston was instrumental in the success of the Florida division of the Federal Writers' Project, a part of President Roosevelt's Works Progress Administration. Their work is why we still have the songs, narratives, and backstories of Floridians in small, close-knit rural communities of color during the Great Depression.

Most people don't know she rented an upstairs room at a boardinghouse in St. Augustine in the 1940s while she revised her autobiography, *Dust Tracks in the Road*. According to First Coast News, local authors, and historians, "Someone needs to save Zora Neale Hurston's House from the bulldozer." Although Hurston died in 1960, four years before the Civil Rights Act was passed, St. Augustine was an important factor in that great moral drama that resulted in efforts bending toward equal justice. A museum honoring her work and exploring its impact on the history of the civil rights movement is an immense benefit to future generations.

On the side of the house is a fanciful drawing of Zora, with one of her quotes inscribed: "Love makes your soul crawl out of its hiding place."

Zore Neale Hurston rewrote her autobiography Dust Tracks in the Road *at this boardinghouse.*

Built in 1930, the two-story cement-block-and-stucco house is a National Historic Landmark because of Hurston's work as a writer of the Harlem Renaissance.

ZORA BOARDED HERE

WHAT: Old two-story boardinghouse on West King Street housed a famous author

WHERE: 791 King St.

COST: Free to view the outside

PRO TIP: Zora's home on 791 W King St. is a four-bedroom, two-bath, "fixer-upper" sold in July 2023 for $200,000. The owner is an investor who bought other properties on West King Street.

LINCOLNVILLE MUSEUM AND CULTURAL CENTER

What was the name of the old high school this building used to serve?

An easy walk from the historic district, the Lincolnville Museum and Cultural Center chronicles centuries of African American history. There are maps, portraits, vintage newsreels, and memorabilia from the military, civil rights movement, education, and business history in Lincolnville. The infamous door and lunch counter from Woolworth five and dime on King Street, site of many Freedom sit-ins during the civil rights movement, are on exhibit here, complete with mannequins restaging the events.

The museum is housed in the old Excelsior High School, the first public high school for African Americans in St. Augustine. It operated for 40 years from 1925 to 1968. If you look up just before you walk through the front doors, you notice the words Excelsior High School rounding the arch on the highest wall. The school educated thousands of students who went on to assume leadership roles in the local community and beyond.

DESIGNED BY A FAMOUS ARCHITECT

WHAT: The old Excelsior High School

WHERE: 102 Martin Luther King Jr. Ave.

COST: $10 for adults, $5 for students

PRO TIP: The Friends of Lincolnville is the nonprofit organization that saved the building from demolition and dedicated its support to the museum.

Willie Galimore, an NFL player with the Chicago Bears from 1957 to 1963, attended Excelsior High School.

Top: *The Old Excelsior High School in Lincolnville.*
Right: *The Lincolnville Museum and Cultural
Center.*

Designed by Arhitect Fred A. Henderich of New York, Excelsior
High School is an example of masonry Mediterranean Revival
Architecture. It is on the National Register of Historic Places. Mr.
Henderich is responsible for the design of other local landmarks,
including the St. Augustine Visitor Information Center and the St.
Augustine Record.

The museum is open Tuesday through Saturday 10:30 a.m. to 4:30 p.m.

THE WINDOWS OF FLAGLER COLLEGE

What rare work of art resides within a college cafeteria?

Flagler College is home to the largest collection of Louis Comfort Tiffany stained glass windows. More than 79 windows decorate the dining hall in linear and lattice designs. They are another of St. Augustine's authentic relics from the Gilded Age of the late 19th century. On sunny days, gem-colored light streams through the oval dining hall, drawing attention to murals on the walls and ceiling. The famous stained glass windows can be viewed outdoors on the east side of the building.

American artist Louis Comfort Tiffany is best known for his stained glass, but he also was the first design director of luxury jeweler Tiffany & Co. Although Tiffany's work is associated with the Art Nouveau and Aesthetic movements, he was inspired by the Roman medieval artisan technique of "draped glass." Tiffany created "drapery" glass where the hot glass is folded to mimic the folds of fabric, creating a three-dimensional effect. Tiffany also used copper foil instead of lead to join the stained glass pieces together.

TIFFANY GLASS

WHAT: The Ponce Dining Hall at Flagler College

WHERE: 74 King St.

COST: Free, but only students and families are allowed in the dining hall outside of designated tours. Tours are $16 for ages 4 and up.

PRO TIP: Flagler College was once the Hotel Ponce de León, a luxurious retreat for Northerners who expected the very best.

The Flagler College collection of stained glass is considered to be among Tiffany's best work.

Top: *The dining hall featuring Louis Comfort Tiffany stained glass windows at Flagler College.* Bottom: *This is the exterior view of the windows.*

Appraised at almost four million dollars by the popular PBS television program *Antiques Roadshow* in 2015, the windows preserve their earliest grace and luminescence. Student guides give one-hour tours daily from 10 a.m. to 2 p.m. Virtual tours are available from the Flagler College website.

VILLA ZORAYDA MUSEUM

Who was the northern millionaire who showed Henry Flagler an innovative method of construction?

In 1883, Zorayda Castle was built by Boston millionaire and original owner of the Cordova Hotel, Franklin W. Smith. Intending to use the castle as his winter home, he appropriated the design from the Alhambra Palace in Spain. Made of poured concrete and crushed coquina, Villa Zorayda contained Smith's original art and antique collection representing the Gilded Age. It was the first building constructed of poured concrete, a method Henry Flagler adopted to build his hotels.

Villa Zorayda was Smith's winter home for 20 years. The castle was purchased in 1913 by Abraham Mussallem who was an expert on antique rugs and artifacts. Abraham added some of his priceless artifacts to the collection and, for a while, the ornate establishment was a club and restaurant. In the 1920s, it transformed into a casino and speakeasy. By 1933, the Mussallem family turned it into a museum to benefit the community.

According to the Villa Zorayda website, "One of our most discussed pieces on display is the 'Sacred Cat Rug' which is over

Franklin W. Smith's "winter" home

2400 years old and made from the hairs of ancient cats that roamed the Nile River." The museum also features handmade inlaid furniture from the far corners of world. Villa Zorayda is still owned by the Mussallem family. The museum was closed for eight years starting in 2000 to undergo an extensive renovation to preserve its unique architecture. Today, everyone can view its history and treasures on 45- to 60-minute public tours.

The Villa Zorayda Museum is on the National Register of Historic Places.

SMITH'S CASTLE

WHAT: An ornate Moorish Revival castle

WHERE: 83 King St.

COST: $14.91 for adults, $7.46 for children

PRO TIP: Franklin W. Smith wrote a book about architecture and ancient civilizations based on his travels titled *Design and Prospectus.*

Zorayda means kind, enormous, and dynamic in Arabic.

CORNER MARKET

Where is the only business owned by an African American in Lincolnville?

A few blocks south of historic downtown is another stroll through St. Augustine's past. Rich in history and culture, Lincolnville is a neighborhood settled in 1866 by former slaves. Years later, one of its families, the Smiths, opened the Corner Market on Martin Luther King Boulevard (then called Central Avenue). In the 1920s, it became a library; since integration, the library on Ponce de León Boulevard serves everyone.

Today, the Corner Market is still owned by the Smiths, and it is the last Black-owned business in Lincolnville, originally an outpost for freed slaves. Nyk Smith, veteran of the civil rights era and Lincolnville native, has tended the store for eight years. Food is her passion, and the store sells organic produce, baked goods, meat pies, and candy and honey made with her favorite vegetable, beets. The Lightner Museum gift shop also carries her chocolate-covered beets.

A GENERATION OF BUSINESS

WHAT: A small family-owned grocery store in Lincolnville

WHERE: 97 Martin Luther King Jr. Ave.

COST: Shop the store, or book for catering services.

PRO TIP: Nyk Smith collects literature about African American history and promotes Black authors. The titles are displayed throughout the Corner Market.

There is a secret near the doorway, hidden under a rug. The initials of the original owner, a Lincolnville businessman named Frederick E. Martin, are etched in cement.

The Corner Market is the last Black-owned business in Lincolnville.

The store sits in an historic district on the National Register of Historic Places; Martin Luther King Jr. visited in the '60s, and there is a photograph of King and Rosa Parks prominently displayed in the storefront windows. It is the last Black-owned business in Lincolnville and a stop on the ACCORD Freedom Trail, which marks prominent locations of the civil rights movement in St. Augustine.

CHILL OUT AT THE ICE PLANT BAR

What remnant of the original ice plant hangs on rails over the bar?

Located close to the San Sebastian River, the Ice Plant Bar was once a 15,000-square-foot power station in the early 1900s, one that eventually became the St. Johns Light and Power Company. The power-driven steam from the machines that generated the electricity was used to make ice. Huge containers froze heavy blocks of ice that were transferred by an overhead bridge crane to conveyances. The huge cubes were smashed and sold to locals and seafood merchants, especially the local shrimpers. By 1927, the building was converted into a real ice plant, and it was the first Florida ice plant to sell quantities of ice for profit.

Advances in refrigeration left the space empty by the 1950s, and it sat vacant for over half a century until its present reincarnation began in 2011. Today, the building is an eclectic happy hour spot in an Art Deco building with geometric lines, double-hung windows, and concrete ornamentation that resembles a palatable factory. The original crane once used to lift the ice blocks is located over the bar.

Owned by former St. Augustine Amphitheatre general manager, Ryan Dettra, since 2010, the bar features a full locavore lunch, dinner, and craft cocktail menu. They even serve brunch. It doesn't

A RESTORED STRUCTURE

WHAT: Former utility and ice plant building in the early 20th century

WHERE: 110 Riberia St.

COST: The tour is free. Cocktails are around $15, meals range from $12 to $39.

PRO TIP: The building is listed on the National Register of Historic Places.

get much better than sitting in the Ice Plant Bar over blue crab beignets sipping a Bad Moon Rising. And according to Dettra, his ice cubes are perfect.

Restoration of the old ice plant cost close to $3 million.

An old ice plant is converted into a neighborhood bar next to a distillery.

OLD ST. JOHNS COUNTY JAIL

Why is the old jail pink?

Take one look at the Old St. Johns County Jail, and it should surprise no one that Henry Flagler, the expansive 19th-century mentor of St. Augustine tourism and hospitality, was involved in its design. When he planned the Hotel Ponce de León on King Street, it was located right next to the local jail. He had it torn down because he needed the land and didn't want his luxury hotel to have a view of hangings. He financed a new jail in 1891, built by the P. J. Pauly Jail Building and Manufacturing Company in the Romanesque Revival style of architecture. Flagler wanted the jail to blend in with Victorian-era architecture, hence its rosy-colored appearance. Its appearance was deceptive.

Sheriff Joe Perry was the warden for the offenders housed in the St. Johns County Jail. He and his family lived in an apartment adjoining the detention home. Perry stood six feet, six inches and weighed over 300 pounds, an obvious deterrent to rambunctious prison behavior. By all accounts, prisoners under his watch did not rebel, but they did not reform or thrive either. One of Perry's

The Old Jail Museum offers ghost tours at night with spectral tales of doors slamming and the ghostly sightings of Joe Perry.

80

The Old St. Johns Historical Jail is a pink building designed by Henry Flagler.

favorite methods of discipline was called "the Bird Cage" The metal cage hanging from a rod where prisoners were locked up for hours or days is now a tourist attraction. The museum also displays a whipping post, a replica of the original gallows, and the bleak cells where prisoners languished.

The museum was a working jail until 1953. Today, it is on the National Register of Historic Places.

MANLY PORTABLE CONVICT CAR

How many mules does it take to haul this cage of convicts?

In 1877, the Florida governor, George Franklin Drew, was a Democrat who believed in education. During the Civil War, he sided with the Union despite living in one of the first states to secede. His governor bid was supported by recently freed African Americans because he treated them with respect. He inherited a budget deficit from the previous administration, so to raise funds, he closed the state prison and started a convict leasing program.

This was where the Manly Portable Convict Car came in. There were different sizes, but an average car weighed about two tons and required up to six mules to pull it. It was advertised as "The Car That Has Made Possible the Economic, Safe, and Humane Housing of Convicts at Night on Public Road Work." Sometimes, labor assignments took the convict car too far away to return to the jail by nightfall.

CAMPING FOR CONVICTS

WHAT: Jail on wheels

WHERE: In front of the Old Jail Museum at 167 San Marco Ave.

COST: Free

PRO TIP: The Dalton, Georgia, company called Manly Jail Works that created the cage for convicts also built complete jails on land.

Many other Southern states employed the Manly Portable Convict Car to use for imprisoned men to complete overnight road work. Generally, these were prisoners who had light sentences.

Top: *Exterior of Manly Portable Convict Car.* Inset: *Kiosk explaining the Manly Portable Convict Car.*

Prisoners slept in bunk beds and lit a fire in a barrel for heat. If it was cold, the cage was covered with canvas. The captive men enjoyed advertised "perfect sanitation" because of the openings between the bars. The Manly Jail Works company assured buyers that "a bucket of disinfectant once or twice a month and a bucket of paint a year will keep the cage absolutely clean, sanitary and vermin proof."

GATOR BOB'S OLD ST. AUGUSTINE HISTORY MUSEUM

What precious metals from the Spanish galleons are housed here?

Most who visit the Old St. Augustine History Museum are tourists waiting for the next stop on the Old Town Trolley Tour. If you need to buy a ticket, you wait in line at the gift shop. Why bother? What relics of history could the small museum possibly possess?

To everyone's surprise, the museum is organized and interesting. There are many paintings of local landscapes and photographs of the old hotels; the Alcazar swimming pool is featured in one. The exhibits take you through a chronological order of St. Augustine history, a timeline from the Native Americans to Spanish occupations, the Seminole Indian Wars to the Civil War, the Gilded Age to modern St. Augustine. One exhibit is a fair replica of a Timucuan American Indian village.

There are relics from the Spanish eras occupying St. Augustine, including the gold "fingers" used as currency. An exhibit that features an "Authentic Silver Bar" has a sign that dares visitors to lift all 66.2 pounds of treasure. The bar isn't tethered to anything. If you succeed in lifting it, you're supposed to put it back. The convict reenactors from the Old Jail next door like to give it a try.

You can park at the Old Jail next door.

Top: *Entrance to Gator Bob's Old St. Augustine History Museum*. Inset: *Exhibit of Spanish gold used as currency during the colonial period.*

NEXT TO THE OLD JAIL

WHAT: A museum with a chronological history of St. Augustine and a loose bar of silver

WHERE: 11 Estey St.

COST: $8.50; free for kids under 3 and those with a trolley ticket

PRO TIP: It takes about 45 minutes to an hour to tour the museum.

POTTER'S WAX MUSEUM

What was the inspiration for Potter's St. Augustine wax museum?

Although it is the oldest wax museum in the country, it moved around a lot within a local perimeter. A Potter patriarch founded Potter's Wax Museum in St. Augustine in 1887. The historic district on St. George Street burned down, and Potter's relatives relocated the museum twice on King Street. It closed in 1970, and the 200 wax figures were auctioned off.

A former curator bought the wax mannequins and reopened the museum in 1987. Today, the wax museum on Orange Street sits at the intersection of the former Cubo and Rosario line that helped protect St. Augustine from invaders. Potter's Wax Museum is distinct from others (such as Madame Tussauds, which inspired it) because it features Florida history along with 160 of the usual posturing wax suspects: European monarchs, pop stars, and torture chamber denizens.

The wax museum is housed in the authentic Old Drug Store, the oldest in Florida, which today exhibits the kind of snake oil remedies and pomades popular in the 18th and 19th centuries. In 1739, 49-year-old Confederate soldier Thomas William Speissegger bought it. The old Speissegger

---

WAX REPLICAS AND DRUG STORE RELICS

WHAT: Wax Museum and Old Drug Store

WHERE: 31 Orange St.

COST: $18.99, free for children under 3

PRO TIP: George Potter used to live in the house that is now O. C. White's Seafood and Spirits.

A statue of Henry Flagler lounges on a bench outside the wax useum.

A seated statue of Henry Flagler lounges in front of Potter's Wax Museum.

Drugstore was maintained until the 1960s by the reclusive and eccentric Speissegger brothers (Thomas's sons) who lived above the store. Most locals swear it is haunted.

It is a Florida Heritage Site, sponsored by Historic Tours of America and the Florida Department of State.

BLUEBIRD OF HAPPINESS AT VILANO BEACH

What color was the bluebird before it was painted?

For over a decade, Vilano Beach has hosted its own widely recognized landmark: a Bluebird of Happiness on the public pier. Like the Southernmost Point Buoy in Key West, the eight-foot fiberglass sculpture of a bluebird is iconic to the region. Created for the "Happiness is" campaign, it represents joy and positivity.

The bluebird was around in the 1940s, although it was a bird of a different hue. Originally orange, it was used to advertise orange juice at a citrus shop. In the 1970s, the Florida Citrus Commission marketed the slogan "Happiness Is Florida Orange Juice," which was promoted by brand ambassador and singer Anita Bryant.

Then it was painted blue for a new owner who ran a motel, and in the 1960s, a public art campaign and "Bring Back the Bird" movement restored the Bluebird of Happiness to its rightful perch. Obviously, this was a happy ending because the bird was completely restored and

AN 84-YEAR-OLD PHOTO OP

WHAT: Bluebird beach icon

WHERE: At the end of Vilano Road

COST: Free

PRO TIP: There are numerous banners of the bluebird leading up to the actual statue at the Vilano Beach Public Pier. Enjoy the Vilano Beach Market Walk every third Saturday from 4 to 8 p.m. offering produce, art, and crafts.

The "Happiness" slogan for the Bluebird goes back to the 1970 advertising campaign: "Happiness Is Florida Orange Juice."

The Bluebird of Happiness at Vilano Beach pier inspires visitors to take selfies.

now resides as a familiar figure photo op on the pier. On the base of its stand are the names of donors and the following message:

"The 'Bluebird,' an iconic symbol nostalgic of the early traveling days to Florida (circa 1950), was a roadside attraction. Happiness is being in Vilano. Project sponsored by Vilano Beach Main Street and North Shores Improvement Association, dedicated June 1, 2013."

LOVE TREE AT THE BAR HARBOR CHEESECAKE COMPANY

Where does a kiss guarantee true love forever?

Bar Harbor Cheesecake Company opened its first location in Maine in 2019; one year later, it landed in St. Augustine in a location that has a verifiable Love Tree on the front lawn. Many businesses have come and gone in this spot, but the Love Tree remains eternal.

This symbol of love is a palm tree growing out of an oak tree. Although unusual, a palm seed can send down shallow roots that don't interfere with the oak's growth. According to legend, one lover planted the oak tree and one the palm tree. When the two trees fused, its powers granted eternal love and fidelity to all who kiss beneath it. Proposals and weddings are popular under the Love Tree.

Some people believe the legend was made up to lure tourists, while others believe the tree's proximity to the Tolomato Cemetery installed a benevolent spirit within it. Native

A TREE WITH A LEGEND

WHAT: A palm tree growing out of an oak tree

WHERE: 6 Cordova St.

COST: Menu prices range from $10 to $29; the Love Tree is free.

PRO TIP: St. Augustine has seven Love Trees, but the one in front of Bar Harbor Cheesecake Company is the only one that carries the legend.

Ripley's Believe It or Not! features the Love Tree and its legend as one of its oddities.

A kiss under the Love Tree guarantees lasting affection.

St. Augustinians caution tourists to carefully consider with whom they want to spend eternity before sealing their love with a kiss in this iconic spot.

The cheesecake company serves a variety of cheesecake, charcuterie boards, salads, and wraps. It's open from 11 a.m. to 11 p.m. seven days a week, and reservations are accepted. A kiss with your special someone under the Love Tree comes with no charge.

DR. ROBERT B. HAYLING FREEDOM PARK

Who was Dr. Robert Hayling?

A popular dentist and air force veteran, Dr. Robert B. Hayling is known as the father of the civil rights movement in St. Augustine. As the son of a college professor growing up in Florida's capital, Hayling was exposed to political activism at an early age. In St. Augustine, he mobilized young people, mostly students, to peacefully demonstrate for civil rights. Hayling's movement caught fire, and civil rights activists such as Mary Peabody, Andrew Young, Martin Luther King Jr., and others were drawn to the city to help St. Augustine and Dr. Hayling's cause.

In a terrifying struggle against the segregationists, Dr. Hayling and a few associates were attacked at a meeting, beaten, hospitalized, and then charged with assault. Even the signing of the Civil Rights Act in 1964 couldn't heal the wounds of injustice Dr. Hayling suffered. He eventually moved to Cocoa and then Ft. Lauderdale, where he lived until his death in 2015.

HONORING A ST. AUGUSTINE CIVIL RIGHTS MENTOR

WHAT: A park named after a local dentist and civil rights activist

WHERE: 601 Riberia St.

COST: Free

PRO TIP: The park was founded as a remembrance of the civil rights movement and in honor of the man who suffered in bringing the Civil Rights Act of 1964 to fruition.

Dr. Hayling died in Broward County, 51 years after the passage of the Civil Rights Act.

Freedom Park in Lincolnville, named after the father of the civil rights movement in St. Augustine

Today, Freedom Park, near the Matanzas River, is named in Dr. Hayley's honor for his role in bringing civil rights to a deeply Southern city. It is a park of reflection as well as recreation as evidenced by the Freedom Memorial, which functions as a 10-foot chime.

ACCORD CIVIL RIGHTS MUSEUM

What personal artifacts of Dr. Hayling's are still in the museum?

The ACCORD (Anniversary to Commemorate the Civil Rights Demonstrations, Inc.) Civil Rights Museum is located in Lincolnville at the site of Dr. Robert Hayling's former dental office. Hayling was the second Black dentist in St. Augustine, and the first Black dentist voted into the American Dental Association in 1960. Hayling's office held the first integrated waiting room in St. Augustine. His dental chair and equipment are still there.

Dr. Hayling was present at the dedication of the museum.

An old dental office is now a civil rights museum.

Hayling was known as the leader of the local civil rights movement in St. Augustine. Martin Luther King Jr. discussed strategy in this office, and young people were recruited for sit-ins and marches there. History was made, and social change began.

Opened in 2014, a half century after the passage of the Civil Rights Act, the ACCORD museum holds artifacts from the struggles of integration in the 1960s. It provides daily film viewings of civil rights documentaries, and there are pictures, letters, books, newspaper headlines, and TV clips verifying the role St. Augustine played in the civil rights movement. It's one of the few museums to document the tribulations of the St. Augustine Four, a quartet of Black teens who ordered lunch from a stool at Woolworth and consequently served six months of hard time. They were released after the intervention of Dodgers infielder Jackie Robinson.

The museum is open by appointment and is available as a venue for lectures and events.

DR. HAYLING'S DENTAL OFFICE

WHAT: Museum in Lincolnville documenting the civil rights struggle of the 1960s in St. Augustine.

WHERE: 79 Bridge St.

COST: Donations accepted.

PRO TIP: The museum is a stop on the ACCORD Freedom Trail.

SAINT PAUL'S AME CHURCH

How old is this historic church?

Saint Paul African Methodist Episcopal (AME) Church on MLK Jr. Avenue (formerly Central Avenue) opened in its current building in 1902 after struggling to find a permanent home since its founding in 1873. Yellow fever, a meager congregation, bankruptcy, and eviction did not deter the faithful or make them less persistent in establishing their goal. As tourism grew in the city of St. Augustine, so did the AME church. Newcomers diluted the Spanish era's influence of the Catholic church, and AME membership soared.

The church was a refuge for the civil rights movement in St. Augustine in the 1960s. Martin Luther King Jr. and Andrew Young spoke at its pulpit; it's the only place where King ever spoke

Saint Paul AME Church where Dr. Martin Luther King Jr. preached in 1963

and consequently led a march. All marches for equal rights in St. Augustine began and ended at Saint Paul.

It is an early-20th-century red brick building designed in the style of Gothic Revival with hexagonal stained glass windows, a spire, and a pointed arch over the door. Today, outside of normal worship activities, Saint Paul also sponsors speakers, art shows, and concerts. Down the street is the old Excelsior High School, now the Lincolnville Museum and Cultural Center, and across the street is one of the oldest continuous Catholic churches in the county, St. Benedict the Moor. Surrounded by history and once the hub of social change, the AME church earned its place in the Lincolnville Historic District on the National Register of Historic Places.

LINCOLNVILLE'S FAMOUS CHURCH

WHAT: Church headquarters for Martin Luther King Jr. in 1964

WHERE: 85 Martin Luther King Jr. Ave.

COST: Donations accepted

PRO TIP: Services are available virtually.

2023 marks the 150th year anniversary of Saint Paul, established in 1873.

ACCORD FREEDOM TRAIL

What is the Freedom Trail in St. Augustine?

Boston has a Freedom Trail commemorating sites of important events and battles in the Revolutionary War. St. Augustine has a Freedom Trail too, honoring another important American battle for independence. The Freedom Trail was a project incorporated in 2004 to document the historic events in St. Augustine that led to the Civil Rights Act of 1964. Established by the Anniversary to Commemorate the Civil Rights Demonstrations Inc. (ACCORD), it includes 31 historical markers at important locations. A comprehensive listing, along with a description of each location, is available on the website.

The trail is relatively chronological, starting from the origin of the St. Augustine movement and including people and places that influenced the passage of the Civil Rights Act. It begins on Lincolnville's Bridge Street, where Dr. Hayling,

THE ST. AUGUSTINE CIVIL RIGHTS TRAIL

WHAT: A walk through historic St. Augustine honoring events of the civil rights movement

WHERE: It begins at 79 Bridge St. A full list of sites can be found at accordfreedomtrail.org.

COST: Free

PRO TIP: At King's invitation, Jackie Robinson, second baseman for the Dodgers, spoke at the Lincolnville AME church (a stop on the Freedom Trail) to a crowd of 600 in 1964.

Civil rights activist Andrew Young went on to become a United States Ambassador to the United Nations and the 55th mayor of Atlanta.

Top: *All that is left of a home on West King Street torched by the Ku Klux Klan in 1963.* Inset: *A kiosk explaining the Freedom Trail in St. Augustine.*

the father of the St. Augustine civil rights movement, practiced dentistry and met with young demonstrators. It meanders through the old neighborhood, identifying prominent Lincolnville businesses, churches, athletes, headquarters of the Southern Christian Leadership Conference, Ku Klux Klan activity, homes of the "St. Augustine Four" (teens sent to prison for ordering lunch at Woolworth), and many more memorials of living history. Even the Plaza de la Constitución marks the bronze footsteps of the Andrew Young Crossing where the young integrationist marched for civil rights.

MLK JR.'S STEPS AT THE HILTON HISTORIC BAYFRONT HOTEL

What famous civil rights struggle occurred on the grounds of this hotel?

While Martin Luther King Jr. was in St. Augustine in the 1960s, he participated in protests and sit-ins to advance the fight for equality. He stayed in Lincolnville, the historic neighborhood founded by freed slaves, shuffling from house to house to remain discreet since his life was always in danger. Segregationists often rode through the streets of Lincolnville, shooting into homes.

In what some say was a symbolic gesture, King attempted to join friends for lunch in the segregated Monson Motor Lodge, now the Bayfront Hilton downtown. He was arrested and jailed. He wrote a letter from jail to a rabbi who supported civil rights, encouraging him to take action. He and a group of rabbis organized a sit-in at the

A REMNANT OF SEGREGATION

WHAT: The steps where MLK Jr. stood when he was arrested in 1964

WHERE: 32 Avenida Menéndez

COST: Free

PRO TIP: The Bayfront Hilton is renowned for its Christmas decorations during the Nights of Lights festival from November through January.

An incident at Monson Motor Lodge made international news in 1964 when owner James Brock poured acid into the swimming pool attempting to remove a group of activists.

Steps where Martin Luther King Jr. was arrested at the former Monson Motor Lodge, now the Bayside Hilton.

motel a week later and were consequently arrested; it was the largest arrest of rabbis in American history.

The Monson Motor Lodge was torn down in 2003, but the steps where King was arrested are still there, along with a plaque that displays the following:

> *These steps were salvaged when the Monson Motel was demolished in 2003 and remain in tribute to Dr. Martin Luther King, Jr. who was arrested here in 1964.*

There is a commemorative plaque at the Hilton for the rabbis as well.

ATHALIA PONSELL LINDSLEY HOUSE ON MARINE STREET

Where is the scene of the most famous unsolved murder in St. Augustine?

On January 23, 1974, Athalia Ponsell Lindsley was nearly decapitated on the steps leading up to her Marine Street mansion. It was 6 p.m., suppertime, yet a crowd quickly gathered, and someone draped a sheet over her body. Athalia's husband, former St. Augustine mayor James Lindsley, showed up with his lawyer, and Sheriff Dudley Garrett Jr. arrived too late to keep an ambulance driver from spraying down the bloody driveway, destroying evidence.

The case was never officially solved, although if you mention the murder to any long-term St. Augustinian, they'll tell you who did it. Almost everyone who lived there at the time had a relative or a friend connected to the case, either professionally or personally. Time also lent a more objective rendering of the evidence.

Athalia's next-door neighbor, Alan Stanford, was brought to trial for the murder. He was a bureaucrat, an Episcopalian usher, husband, father, and a man whose motive for murder could have been that he had good reason to suspect Athalia's complaints were the reason his job was threatened. He was acquitted.

His church raised money for his defense. The mood of some city residents, who disapproved of Athalia's outspoken demeanor, seemed to indicate that she'd gotten what she deserved. The case crossed from private tragedy into public drama, where its relevance resides to this day. Part of the public fascination with this true crime

---

Before new housing construction on Marine Street in 2016, Athalia's mansion had a view of Matanzas Bay.

The house on Marine Street where a notorious true crime occurred

SITE OF A TRUE-CRIME MURDER

is not its missing pieces and the lack of a murder conviction. It's that it happened at all, and that whoever did it got away with murder.

There are True Crime Tours in St. Augustine that take you past the Marine Street abode. It's an easy walk from O. C. White's Seafood and Spirits.

WHAT: Scene of a famous true-crime murder

WHERE: 124 Marine St.

COST: Free

PRO TIP: The house is privately owned but displays the same symmetrical design and house color it had in the 1970s.

DAVID AT RIPLEY'S BELIEVE IT OR NOT!

What replica of a famous statue initially caused a traffic jam on San Marco Avenue?

On the west side of Ripley's Believe It or Not! Odditorium, is a replica of Michelangelo's statue of David. The Italian Renaissance sculptor and painter created the original 17-foot statue in 1504 located in Florence, Italy. This replica of *David*, which displayed at the 1964 New York World's Fair, resided in California before arriving in St. Augustine in 2007.

Apparently, the sculptors from the Sollazzini and Sons Studio of Florence used one monumental piece of marble as Michelangelo did, quarried from the same site in Tuscany, Italy. Showing a pensive David before he wields his southpaw slingshot, the statue's nudity represents his youth and innocence. The hand-carved replica weighs an even ton.

Historically, Ripley's four-story, poured concrete, Moorish-designed building was known as Castle Warden. An oil magnate and

AN EXACT REPLICA OF A FAMOUS SCULPTURE

WHAT: Replica of Michelangelo's David

WHERE: 19 San Marco Ave.

COST: Statue is free and outside the museum; tickets for Ripley's are $23.99 for adults, $12.99 for children

PRO TIP: The statue is enclosed by a hedge to shield it from the public eye, but David's head and shoulders can be seen from San Marco Avenue.

Italian artist Donatello sculpted a marble and a bronze *David*, each standing on Goliath's head. His sculpture resides in Florence at the Museo Nazionale del Bargello.

contemporary of Henry Flagler built the colossal structure as a winter home for his wife and 12 children. After he died, the building was a squatting destination for the homeless until Marjorie Kinnan Rawlings bought it in 1941. The *Cross Creek* author transformed it into a hotel, which caught fire in April 1944, killing a dear friend whom Marjorie tried to shelter from domestic abuse. In 1950, the hotel was sold to Ripley's family.

Today, the gallery features more than 300 exhibits.

An amazing replica of Michelangelo's David, surrounded by a hedge, at Ripley's Believe it or Not!

SOUTHERNMOST POINT BUOY REPLICA

Where can you find a replica of a famous Key West tourist prop?

There are many replicas of famous landmarks and works of art in St. Augustine. Portrayed in this book is Michelangelo's famous sculpture of *David*; Villa Zoradaya, modeled after the 13th-century Moorish Alhambra Palace in Spain; and the Medici lions on the Bridge of Lions, which are replicas of famous Italian counterparts.

A replica from the Conch Republic pantomimes its 20-ton concrete Southernmost Point Buoy, which is 90 miles from Cuba. The enormous painted Southern "least" buoy in St. Augustine is the brainchild of prop rental company PRI Productions, Inc. The St. Augustine version marks 470 miles to Cuba rather than the 90 miles from the southernmost point in Key West.

This is a replica of the famous buoy in Key West.

Instead of monopolizing a side street with tourists, this fake buoy hidden outside the St. Augustine Historic District has been relocated to the back of a restaurant property, unobtrusively framed by foliage and a lattice. Unlike the Key West buoy, one of the country's most well-liked and frequently photographed tourist locations, the St. Augustine prop remains low-key and underpromoted. It is a photo op that is readily available to snap, unlike the long lines leading to the real thing almost 400 miles away.

A CONCRETE BUOY REPLICA

WHAT: A replica of Key West's famous Southernmost Point Buoy

WHERE: The Southern "least" buoy in St. Augustine resides, perhaps temporarily, at DJ's Clam Shack at 21 Hypolita St.

COST: Free

PRO TIP: You can find your own replica of the Southernmost Point Buoy online, and there is even a business that specializes in Styrofoam replicas of the famous landmark.

There is a northern "sister buoy" to the Key West buoy in Angle Inlet, Minnesota, erected in 2016, and one in Pennsylvania.

SCHOONER FREEDOM CHARTERS

Where else can you feel like a 19th-century blockade runner?

When in Florida, experience the harbor from the water.

Listed as one of the top 10 attractions in St. Augustine by *USA Today*, the *Schooner Freedom*, a Class B tall ship, has been a family business for 23 years. The ship is a 76-foot steel vessel, and the family is Captain John Zaruba; his wife, Admiral Sarah; and first-mate children Sydney and Jack. The family has navigated thousands of miles on the *Schooner Freedom* and on their private two-masted sailboat. Visitors can join them on daily tours.

Freedom is also a double-masted, gaff-rigged, topsail schooner and the first sailing tour boat certified by the Coast Guard. Sailing on the replica of a 19th-century blockade runner and the only tall ship in St. Augustine seems like a trip back in time. The crew is knowledgeable of historical events, as well as local flora and fauna. Passengers sometimes help the crew hoist sails or even steer at the helm; reviews say it's more of a sailing experience than a tour. *Schooner Freedom* offers daily two-hour day and sunset sails, as well as daily 75-minute

A FAMILY OWNED SAILBOAT TOUR

WHAT: Sail the *Schooner Freedom*

WHERE: 11 Avenida Menéndez

COST: $60 for adults, $45 for children ages 2–16

PRO TIP: Book a trip on the *Schooner Freedom* to view the Nights of Lights, November 18th through January 31.

Captain Jack lets you hoist the sails if it's your birthday.

Schooner Freedom *is the first tall ship expressly designed to carry passengers along the Intercoastal Waterway.* Schooner Freedom *gives a couple of two-hour cruises during the day, a sunset cruise, and a moonlight cruise.*

moonlight sails on Matanzas Bay, along the Intracoastal Waterway. It's the site of numerous proposals, anniversary celebrations, and weddings. Reservations are required.

SOUTH-A-PHILLY STEAKS & HOAGIES

What local store carries a pinball machine players say is "the greatest of all time"?

The wood-frame building on the east end of King Street dates to 1900 and used to be Potter's Wax Museum. Now it is an event center, a bar, and a South-A-Philly Steaks & Hoagies. The latter serves a decent cheesesteak, which you can eat on a high stool by a picture window and watch the horse-drawn carriages, traffic, and pedestrians of St. Augustine. You even can see the Bridge of Lions and the Plaza de la Constitución from the sandwich shop. But the views and food are not the most interesting things about South-A-Philly. It's Godzilla pinball.

To be more specific, it's the 2021 edition by Stern, Pro Godzilla. There are only about 2,000 of these pinball machines in the world. (The Stern website lists all of the locations.) Pinball vlogs review it as "the pinnacle of pinball art and design," and perhaps "the greatest pinball machine of all time." The back art is Godzilla breathing steam while fighting monsters and aliens. The colorful game includes flashing lights, a miniature Godzilla and Mega Godzilla, and a motorized skyscraper building bash toy that collapses. And of course there are the requisite ramps, spinners, magna grabs, and loop shots. The mechanism is flawless, including the third flipper.

Blue Oyster Cult plays the Godzilla theme song at winning intervals along with video clips and authentic Godzilla roars from years of film history. Godzilla Premier and Godzilla LE have more bells and whistles, but Pro is essentially the same game.

Keith Elwin, game designer for Stern Pinball, is responsible for creating the Godzilla versions.

Left: *South-A-Philly Steaks & Hoagies is located on King Street where the old Potter's Wax Museum stood in the late 1940s.* Right: *Play Godzilla Pro pinball and enjoy Godzilla roars and Blue Oyster Cult soundtrack.*

CHEESESTEAK AND GODZILLA PINBALL

WHAT: Godzilla Pro pinball

WHERE: 1 King St.

COST: $8 for a cheesesteak, $1 per game for pinball

PRO TIP: Pinball arcade apps on Amazon run tabs on your games.

There are other pinball games at South-A-Philly like Ninja Turtles and Stranger Things, but for true pinball variety, go to Anastasia Island's Sarbez! (see page 118). It also has Godzilla Pro, although elbow to elbow with other games. At South-A-Philly, Godzilla Pro is set off by itself as it should be.

I SCREAM, YOU SCREAM FOR MAYDAY HANDCRAFTED ICE CREAMS

What does the word "Mayday" have to do with ice cream?

If it seems nothing in St. Augustine is immune to creative expression, you're right. St. Augustine native Stephen DiMare, owner of Mayday Handcrafted Ice Creams, creates a blissful product rife with flavor and originality. Try the Queen Salted Caramel, made with caramelized sugar and flakes of pink Himalayan sea salt. Or the seasonal Ginger Peach ice cream sandwich. Even the seemingly simple Triple Vanilla boasts beaucoup vanilla bean paste. Mayday has homemade sprinkles, too—not the waxy kind!

The name of the shop, Mayday, is a meaningful moniker taken from the tales of American bombardiers during World War II. The temperatures were freezing at the

THE BOMBADIERS' ICE CREAM LEGACY

WHAT: An historical name for an ice-cream store

WHERE: 1765 Tree Blvd. and 100 St. George St.

COST: $3.50 to $8

PRO TIP: Aside from the ice cream made by the bombardiers, the military spent $1 million on a floating ice-cream factory.

Mayday owner Stephen DiMare is something of a Renaissance figure in St. Augustine. He also owns the Hyppo Gourmet Ice Pops, he speaks Italian, and he created a board game called Black Hole Rainbows.

Named after a World War II recipe, Mayday's handcrafted ice cream is worth a scream or two.

high altitudes the men flew, so they began taking buckets of cream and sugar into the gunner area. Air turbulence churned it. If they returned to the hangar, there was Mayday ice cream.

Many soldiers were still in their teens, a time of mass caloric consumption. Ice cream was the military's secret weapon during World War II, ensuring soldiers had enough calories to march.

Although it's no longer churned by bombardiers at atmospheric levels, St. Augustine makes certain that civilians have access to the frozen treat at two locations; one is in historic downtown across from Columbia Restaurant and another is in midtown on Tree Boulevard. They are open seven days a week.

POP INTO THE HYPPO GOURMET ICE POPS SHOP

How did the Hyppo pop shop get its name?

University of Florida grad and owner of the Hyppo Gourmet Ice Pops, Stephen DiMare, says he figured out the flavors for his homemade ice pops during a boring winter in Montana. Almost 15 years later, the shop has sold millions of pops containing no preservatives or anything artificial. The gourmet ice pops shop makes all of its products with fresh fruit; the 500 flavors rotate with the seasons. Try Florida favorites Dragonfruit, Prickly Pear, Muscadine Plum, and Sapodilla. There is nothing like a Cucumber Lemon Mint pop on a blazing summer day in St. Augustine. If you're looking for a refreshing and unique treat, Hyppo is worth checking out!

Where did the weird name come from? There's a Hypolita Street downtown, which may have something to do with it. However, locals know "Hyppo" refers to Saint Augustine of Hippo, for whom the city was named. On August 28, 1585, the feast day of St. Augustine, Spanish admiral Don Pedro Menéndez de Avilés first

ICE POPS THAT POP

WHAT: The Hyppo Gourmet Ice Pops

WHERE: 70 St. George St. and 48 Charlotte St.

COST: $4 to $10

PRO TIP: There are Hyppo and Mayday trucks that drive around neighborhoods during the day, selling ice pops and ice cream to residents.

The world's largest ice pop, made in the Netherlands, weighed 10 tons.

114

Named after the patron saint of St. Augustine, Hyppo's gourmet ice pops just pop with flavor.

spied land. He consequently named it St. Augustine, who was also the patron saint of his hometown of Avilés, Spain. The patronage seems to work; the ice pop shop is lauded in publications such as *USA Today* and *Southern Living*.

Open seven days a week, you can get your fix at two locations downtown. Want to enjoy them at home? Shipping is free on orders of 24 pops or more.

MICRO MASTERPIECES ART GALLERY

What is micro art?

Micro art is a fine-art form of various mediums made on a micro scale, requiring fewer resources and less space. At the Micro Masterpieces Art Gallery, the works of art aren't visible to the human eye; patrons must view them under a lighted microscope.

Miniscule art is so hard to create that there are few artists in the entire world who do it. The owner of the gallery is a collector with hundreds of pieces, mostly from Ukrainian artists. He rotates his tiny exhibition, displaying 30 canvases at a time in his museum. Each sample is around two millimeters in width, the same as a toothpick. Artists use one hair of a paint brush to color their masterpieces. There are also tiny replica sculptures created in the eyes of needles, including a parade of elephants, a parade of camels, a scorpion, a violin, and a gun.

Other samples of tiny art include a sculpture of a flea wearing a bow tie and shoes and renderings of movie stars, musicians, writers, statues, birds, equestrians, and instruments. Local landmarks

A TINY GALLERY

WHAT: Miniscule art under a microscope

WHERE: 100 St. George St.

COST: $10 for adults, $6 for children

PRO TIP: The gallery shares a gift shop with the Medieval Torture Museum on the same floor, but there are two separate entrances—a good thing to know if you have children!

British sculptor Willard Wigam is acknowledged as one of the foremost micro artists of the 21st century.

View micro masterpieces through a microscope.

are represented, such as the St. Augustine coat of arms and the St. Augustine Lighthouse, designed on a fishhook.

At the Micro Masterpieces Art Gallery, it's the little things that matter.

SARBEZ!

What does Sarbez! spell backwards?

Over the Bridge of Lions toward the beach, there is a place where you can score a gourmet grilled cheese sandwich and craft beer to slosh it down. A place with live music, local art, pool, darts, game consoles, and an arcade. This place has a laid-back atmosphere and loose reins on formal etiquette. It's Sarbez!, a one-story building that has been in St. Augustine for over a decade. Locals love it.

Owner and former New Yorker Ryan Kunsch is a fine-arts graduate of Flagler College. Like most grads, he grew fond of his adopted city and didn't want to leave. So, at 22,

Oprah has her own bathroom at Sarbez! Sarbez! is a pinball arcade within the walls of oddly cojoined rooms.

he used the name of his designer clothing line, Sarbez (zebras spelled backward) to open the bar and café specializing in build-your-own grilled cheese and craft beer. Open seven days a week, the venue hosts award events, after-parties, open-mic nights, and trivia.

The collage-like structure is a series of rooms filled with oddities, pinball machines, arcade games, simulation racers, and a lunch counter. There is a tiny plastic zebra perched on a high beam. Best of all, Oprah has not left the building. (Just check out the bathroom in the farthest corner back.)

Look for your old favorites on the wall of tape cassettes.

CONVENE AT CAP'S ON THE WATER

What's so special about *this* seafood restaurant amid so many in St. Augustine?

According to Tripadvisor, Cap's on the Water ranks ninth among the 15 most beautiful restaurants in the US. There is a large wooden outdoor dock with a tiki hut looking out at the Intercoastal Waterway. This is where guests can catch the sunset and cultivate a decidedly mellow mood. Ospreys land in nearby foliage, and sailboats drift in the distance. Serving coastal cuisine right on the Intercoastal, this romantic spot is perfect for proposals and anniversary dinners.

Wine Spectator magazine has awarded Cap's extensive and renowned wine list as "best of" since 2018. The she crab soup and garlic oysters are meals in themselves. If you have room, the desserts are exquisite Florida fare, such as banana pudding, coconut cake, and a Key lime cup.

Owners Bernard and Vivian De Raad bought the old fish camp 21 years ago and quickly raised the rank of the restaurant. They don't take reservations, and the line of cars waiting for valet service can

A POPULAR RESTAURANT

WHAT: One of the best views of the sunset and wild birds on the Intercoastal Waterway

WHERE: 4325 Myrtle St., Vilano Beach

COST: Menu items range from $9 to $59

PRO TIP: You can get the best pictures from the tiki hut. The Fish House restaurant on Riberia Street also provides spectacular sunsets for photographers.

Locals in St. Augustine shorten the seafood restaurant's name to "Cap's," as in "See ya at Cap's."

Cap's on the Water, a popular seafood restaurant, may have the best view of the sunset and birdlife in St. Augustine.

lengthen quite a bit. However, there are three bars and a retail shop in which to while away some time. And, of course, there is always the glorious sunset, one of the best in St. Augustine. Relax. Cap's, like the whitecaps on the Intercoastal, is open seven days a week.

WHETSTONE CHOCOLATES' ORIGINAL CHOCOLATE TOUR

If someone asked if you wanted to book a chocolate tasting tour, what would you say?

If your answer is yes, here's your chance. Whetstone Chocolates of St. Augustine conducts tasting tours with a walk through the factory. But instead of Oompa-Loompas, Whetstone has knowledgeable chocolatiers sharing wisdom about the history of chocolate, the chocolate-making process, and Whetstone's particular role in that narrative.

The love of chocolate is a family affair. Founders Henry and Esther Whetstone were Florida natives, and their daughter Virginia was part of the family business from the time she was in school. Whetstone declares their chocolates are unique because of the ingredients and how they are made, all based on old family recipes and traditions. During the tour, hairnets and beard guards are distributed, and participants learn and taste the differences between milk, dark, and white chocolate made at the production facility. The guides are entertaining, and everyone gets five to six pieces to sample and a $2 off coupon toward a purchase.

FOR CHOCOLATE LOVERS

WHAT: Whetstone's Chocolates' tasting tour

WHERE: Starts at 139 King St.

COST: $10.95 for adults; $8.95 for ages 5 to 17; children under 5 are free

PRO TIP: Tours are offered every day, but it's best to schedule Tuesday through Saturday. The employees are off on Sunday and Monday so you can't see the chocolate going into the molds on the conveyor belts.

Whetstone Chocolates offers tours of its chocolate factory.

The shop features glass counters, bins, and jars filled with delectable chocolates, as well as wrapped gift boxes. There are three locations, including the historic district, Anastasia Island, and the King business district. Rated No. 2 on Tripadvisor's list of St. Augustine attractions, the factory is open seven days a week from 10 a.m. to 10 p.m. Tours run as late as 3:30 p.m.

Eating dark chocolate lowers risk factors for heart disease.

SAN SEBASTIAN WINERY

Where is the "sister" winery to San Sebastian?

Across the street from Carmelo's Marketplace and Flagler dorms is one of Henry Flagler's old East Coast railway buildings known since 1996 as San Sebastian Winery. It is the second-largest winery in Florida. Gary Cox founded the family business, which is the sister winery to Lakeridge Winery & Vineyards in Clermont, which is the largest winery in Florida. In keeping with tradition, San Sebastian grows muscadine grapes from its native region of origin.

The grapes, cultivated 400 years ago by the French Huguenots, produce a prodigious variety of tastes, including chardonnay, pinot grigio, petite sirah, sherry, and cabernet sauvignon. Reservations for daytime wine-tasting tours are available every 15 minutes, seven days a week. If it's your birthday or anniversary, the guide gives you a toast.

In addition to tastings, visitors learn about the local wine, from barreling to bottling, on the tour. The winery is a popular attraction in St. Augustine, hosting thousands of visitors each year. Snatch up tempting gift baskets for sale with wine, cheese, biscuits, and

Historians contend that St. Augustine is the origin of American wine.

San Sebastian Winery is credited with being one of the first places wine was made in Florida.

chocolate. The Cellar Upstairs Bar and Restaurant offers live music and food on the roof Thursday through Sunday. The facility is considered a local secret. It's a spot where visitors can enjoy live music on weekends, along with views of the St. Augustine skyline.

ST. AUGUSTINE BEACH SCULPTURE GARDEN

Where did this artwork come from?

It's easy to miss the sculpture garden. It's a neighbor to the St. Augustine Beach Police Department and the city hall building on A1A South. There is a veterans memorial in the corner of the park with the names of St. Augustine Beach soldiers of every rank and insignia. Beyond that is Lake Anhinga, rife with turtles and, since this is Florida, probably an alligator or two. But it is the sculptures that command visitors' attention. Sculptures worth millions of dollars. Sculptures that weigh tons.

They are made of stone, set out on grassy knolls on pedestals that mark the title and artist. The artist's name that appears most frequently is Thomas Glover W. He and his wife are the founders of the St. Augustine Beach Sculpture Garden and its largest contributors, although others are included on a plaque. There are over a dozen large sculptures, all of them breathtaking works of art. Glover's favorite sculptor was Michelangelo, and his work shows the master's influence.

Glover, Italian born, was adopted by American parents and grew up in the Midwest. He became a renowned sculptor and local artist, and in 2006, he tried to gift the city of St. Augustine with 12 sculptures, half of them his. City officials accepted, but wrangling ensued, and Glover rescinded his offer. In 2009, Glover made the same offer to the city of St. Augustine Beach, and it accepted. The

---

Thomas Glover W. sculpted a piece called *Beaufort Mermaid* in spite of, or perhaps because of, the renowned Thomas Glover of the 17th century who sighted the "first mermaid" on the Rappahannock River in Virginia.

result was the culmination of a lifelong dream of the talented artist.

Glover died of a brain tumor in 2012, but his works of art still reside in a peaceful outdoor landscape. Outdoor sculpture gardens are all the rage at museums. Thanks to a local artist's vison, St. Augustine Beach has one of its own

AN OUTDOOR ART GALLERY

WHAT: A sculpture garden and veteran's memorial

WHERE: Lakeside Park, 2340 A1A S

COST: Free

PRO TIP: Thomas Glover W. was also a gifted painter and musician.

An outdoor art gallery at sculpture garden. The Lakeside Park location features a veterans memorial in addition to rare sculptures

ST. AUGUSTINE ALLIGATOR FARM ZOOLOGICAL PARK

What fun interactive activity gives visitors to this attraction a new perspective?

Although tourists may refer to the facility as "an alligator farm," the St. Augustine Alligator Farm Zoological Park is an actual zoo accredited by the Association of Zoos and Aquariums. They have a research and conservation center, focusing on alligator, crocodile, and reptile science. The park boasts 24 species of crocodiles and albino alligators. A long list of other animal species makes the zoo their home. A rookery for wild birds resides in the back, a fair distance from the gators and crocs. There are also sloths.

The park has been around a long time. Founded in 1893 as a small museum at the end of Anastasia Island, it moved to State Road 16 where it burned down in 1920 from a lightning strike. Then it was hit by a hurricane, washing away most of the remaining alligators, before establishing its present location.

The zoo features animal shows, interactive exhibits, and four albino alligators. According to zoo director John Brueggen, their

A PLETHORA OF NATIVE FLORIDA WILDLIFE

WHAT: Albino alligators

WHERE: 999 Anastasia Blvd.

COST: $33.99 for adults, $18.99 for children 3–11

PRO TIP: There is a picture of the St. Augustine albino alligator in the Jacksonville Public Library.

The zoo is in a designated US historic district.

A lack of melanin accounts for the rare albino coloring of this alligator at the St. Augustine Alligator Farm Zoological Park.

white coloring is the result of a rare genetic mutation that results in the absence of melanin, a skin pigment.

The zoo is open every day from 9 a.m. to 5 p.m. It has a zip line called the Crocodile Crossing where you can fly over the reptiles.

BIRD ISLAND PARK

Where can you find a park with a rookery, turtles, and native plants?

An agency called the Guana Tolomato Matanzas (GTM) protects conserved land and beaches. Its protective umbrella extends to a place north on A1A called Bird Island Park, which includes a small island and a four-acre park. It's located north of Vilano Beach near the Tolomato River, a southerly border of the National Estuarine Research Reserve.

Adjacent to the Ponte Vedra library, there is a large pond filled with turtles encircling a hedged maze, a nature trail, art, a playground, a pavilion, and species of native plants. It is also a stop on the Great Florida Birding Trail with a rookery that provides a home for wildlife such as double-crested cormorants, egrets, brown pelicans, and great blue herons, among others. The birds roost in the shade trees so it's a favorite spot for birding enthusiasts.

The design was donated by Bobby Weed, best known for designing golf courses. The Ponte Vedra community raised most of the money with help from the St. Johns Tourist Development Council, Friends of the Library, and the Cultural Center of Ponte Vedra Beach. The park opened in 2010.

A PEACEFUL PLACE TO READ

WHAT: A nature trail and a rookery adjacent to the Ponte Vedra library

WHERE: 101 Library Blvd., Ponte Vedra Beach

COST: Free

PRO TIP: The turtles seem quite friendly with each other and often swim together.

Since it's next to a library, Bird Island Park has a peaceful reading area.

Bird Island is a peaceful spot behind the Ponte Vedra library.

The parking lot is at the southern end of the Ponte Vedra library, and the park is open from dawn to dusk, every day.

WEATHERVANE AT HOWARD JOHNSON MOTOR LODGE

What is left to salvage at an abandoned HoJo restaurant?

The old Howard Johnson's restaurant in west St. Augustine on State Road 16 closed in the late 1990s. The parking lot is empty, cracked, and full of potholes. A hurricane could come and blow the property away, and no one would care.

Well, not quite. There is value to behold if you look up to the rooftop. The HoJo's weathervane featuring silhouettes of a nursery rhyme is so unique that there are websites dedicated to it. It tells road-weary travelers that this abandoned restaurant used to be a Howard Johnson's Motor Lodge. How does it do that?

Howard Johnson's weathervanes were constructed to tell potential guests what each complex featured. The weathervane on West 16 displays the restaurant design for a HoJo's Motor Lodge complex, featuring the Pieman, Simple Simon, his dog, and a lamppost from the Mother Goose rhyme. Rarer still is the lamplighter design and the version for the HoJo's stand-alone restaurant. There were earlier varieties of the motor

The last Howard Johnson's restaurant closed in Lake George, New York, in 2022.

lodge weathervane with a 3D lamppost, but hardly anyone is lucky enough to find that one.

Howard Johnson's, the budget hotel with an adjoining restaurant serving 28 flavors of ice cream, is no more. Its weathervane is a symbol of an era when new interstates made travel by car accessible and Simple Simon and the Pieman kept a lamp lit for you.

The HoJo's weathervane is a fast-disappearing icon of the early days of affordable roadside motels.

ST. AUGUSTINE SURF CULTURE & HISTORY MUSEUM

Who knew St. Augustine had such a strong surfing culture?

When people think of St. Augustine, they think of history, ancient history, and ghost history. But surf history? Founded by the St. Augustine Historical Society in 2019 (COVID delayed the opening of the museum until 2021), members conducted interviews with surfers and surf shop owners, similar to the efforts of the Works Progress Administration in rural communities in the 1930s. The historians established a digital surf society on Facebook and an enduring surf culture in the ancient city.

This led to the St. Augustine Surf Culture & History Museum, located in the Tovar House section of the González-Alvarez Oldest House Complex. Sponsored by local surfers and businesses, the museum showcases the contributions of local surfers, who influenced the growth and expertise of surfing in St. Augustine. The community-driven effort recognized Anastasia beaches as the birthplace of contemporary surfing in Florida. The museum celebrates the men and women, boys and girls, who rode the

SURF CULTURE IN ST. AUGUSTINE

WHAT: A museum in the Oldest House Museum Complex dedicated to surfing memorabilia

WHERE: 14 St. Frances St.

COST: $12.95 gets adults into the surf museum, the Oldest House Museum, and on the grounds of the entire complex. Children are $4.95.

PRO TIP: Admission is half off for St. Johns County residents.

This is the only surf museum in Florida.

Top: *The Creature dons surf attire at the St. Augustine Surf Culture & History Museum.* Inset: *The surf museum revives the history of surf culture in its museum within the Oldest House Complex.*

Atlantic waves on surfboards dating back to 1915. Flagler College students were notable enthusiasts; at one time, the college was known as the University of Surf.

The museum displays surfboards, photos, oral histories, surf slang interpretations, and the Creature from the Black Lagoon decked out in striped swim trunks. The incongruous surf display is set against the backdrop of colonial period coquina walls erected in 1763.

It's totally rad. Hang ten, y'all.

OLD SPANISH TRAIL ZERO MILESTONE MARKER

What is the Old Spanish Trail (OST)?

The Spanish colonial influence is everywhere in St. Augustine. From architecture and cobblestone streets to reenactments, cuisine, and Mediterranean culture, it lingers in Florida's oldest continually occupied city. A case in point is the hefty coquina-comprised orb known as the Old Spanish Trail Zero Milestone marker.

It marks the end (or beginning) of the Old Spanish Trail. Close to 2,500 miles in length, the OST linked San Diego on the West Coast to St. Augustine. It trekked through mountainous highs, canyon lows, deserts, and waterways, traversing eight states: Florida, Alabama, Mississippi, Louisiana, Texas, New Mexico, Arizona, and California. It followed the paths of future highways from northeast Florida to the southwestern Pacific Ocean.

The 100-year-old sculpture was erected in 1924 by the Woman's Exchange, a nonprofit organization founded by women in the 19th century (see "The Peña-Peck House Museum"). The trail initially was imagined to expedite goods and services, but it quickly became more of a tourist designation for those in the know. The nonprofit advocated for road trips, when the automobile was still new, to enable families to discover America.

The OST's original claim to follow the same path as the Spanish conquistadors 400 years ago is largely aspirational. The

---

Our highway system began as Indian trails, and the OST is a case in point. It employed a system of paths well known to indigenous tribes.

The Old Spanish Trail Zero Milestone in St. Augustine, is a spherical monument made of coquina.

OST was longer than the Oregon Trail, and parts of it are still accessible. St. Augustine is one of its "centennial cities," designated by the Old Spanish Trail Centennial Celebration Association.

A 100-YEAR-OLD COQUINA SPHERE

WHAT: Old Spanish Trail marker

WHERE: Behind the Visitor Information Center and next to the Huguenot Cemetery

COST: Free

PRO TIP: A zero-mile marker was posted in San Diego the same year as the massive stone orb in St. Augustine. San Diego's marker is located in the downtown Horton Plaza shopping mall.

RIBERA GARDEN

What is the origin of the mysterious fountain in Ribera Garden?

If you've strolled St. George Street, you've likely walked right by it numerous times. Dedicated in 1966, the Ribera Garden aimed to display how Spanish Florida lived during the colonial period. Located next to the Ribera House, the garden was created by St. Augustine Restoration, Inc. and the Florida Federation of Garden Clubs. It was the first formal garden in historic downtown St. Augustine, and its planners researched what plants were known to flourish during colonial times. Included were crinum, canna, firebush, and bamboo.

A broken fountain sits off to the side. It used to have a water jet before the basin split in half. According to Charles Tingley of the St. Augustine Historic Society, colonial St. Augustine did not have fountains, but nevertheless, the fountain is listed in the society's archives, describing" . . . water flows from the mouth of a concrete head into the large ornate rectangular basin below."

A MYSTERIOUS ARTIFACT

WHAT: A broken fountain in the courtyard of the Ribera Garden

WHERE: 22 St. George St.

COST: Free

PRO TIP: Ribera Garden is included in the St. Augustine Town Plan Historic District, which is listed on the National Register of Historic Places.

The Ribera House at 22 St. George St. is a reconstruction of the home that originally stood on this site during the first Spanish period of St. Augustine. It is currently a gift shop managed by the University of Florida.

A broken fountain in Ribera Garden may depict the massacre of the Huguenots and St. Augustine's first Mass.

A mural on the basin depicts a benediction and a beheading, although it's not clear of whom. Tingley suggests a Greco-Roman garden deity. Or it could reflect Admiral Pedro Menéndez's genocidal executions of the French Huguenots and the consequent first Mass in 1565. But no one really knows.

The Ribera Garden was restored in 2019 by the University of Florida Historic St. Augustine board.

PROHIBITION KITCHEN

Does this restaurant still host a speakeasy?

Prohibition Kitchen is a restaurant that looks as though it stepped straight out of the days when alcohol was illegal and lawmakers raided clubs that served it. The two-story stucco-and-concrete building features an interior of reclaimed wood from old barns and buildings, brick walls, and accents such as metal pipes, velvet curtains, and vintage art. The ceiling is made of pressed tin in geometric designs.

The popular restaurant on St. George Street was never an obvious speakeasy. It was a theater owned by a businessman named Bartolo Genovar, who hosted vaudeville, silent movies, and live music. The basement offered sanctuary to drinkers and gamblers, a common sight in St. Augustine during Prohibition.

The Genovar Theater was torn down in the 1970s and rebuilt as a restaurant, retaining its illicit ambiance and reputation as a social hub. It serves high-quality local food, craft beer, and cocktails. Try the Bootlegger Burger!

A POPULAR RESTAURANT WITH A HISTORY

WHAT: A former opera house and speakeasy

WHERE: 121 St. George St.

COST: $7-$35 per person

PRO TIP: Prohibition Kitchen has the longest bar in the city of St. Augustine.

It is rumored that Prohibition Kitchen has a secret entrance to a speakeasy in its basement just like the one that functioned in the 1920s. People claim a secret password is required to enter.

A former speakeasy, Prohibition Kitchen is a popular restaurant on St. George Street.

There is live music every night, and the doors stay open every day from 11:30 a.m. to 10 p.m., 1 a.m. on Saturdays. There is no parking except in the public garage or on a nearby side street.

FLORIDA NATIONAL GUARD HEADQUARTERS

What centuries-old building constructed by Franciscan monks resides in this military facility?

The St. Augustine headquarters for the Florida National Guard is on Marine Street. Naturally, since this is St. Augustine, there is an antique building associated with the military facility. St. Francis Barracks is named in honor of St. Francis of Assisi and is one of the oldest buildings in St. Augustine.

Originally built by Franciscan friars, it was renovated into military barracks by the British in 1763 during their brief occupation. It also served as headquarters for the Confederacy, the Union, and the United States military. Around the turn of the 20th century, Congress ordered Florida to take over the St. Francis Barracks and to begin operations as the State Arsenal and headquarters for the Florida National Guard.

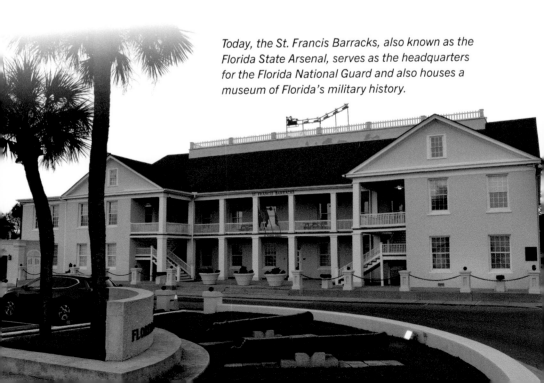

Today, the St. Francis Barracks, also known as the Florida State Arsenal, serves as the headquarters for the Florida National Guard and also houses a museum of Florida's military history.

Why St. Augustine? It was a logical choice for a military outpost. A former colony with deep harbors, it was the capital of Spanish Florida for centuries. The National Guard traces its origin back to the first Spanish settlers organized by the city's forefathers. St. Augustine also has access to the St. Johns River and Intercoastal Waterway. Its position on the Atlantic coast means accessibility to larger cities such as Jacksonville and Orlando.

Comprised of nearly 10,000 soldiers, today's Florida National Guard units in St. Augustine provide for public safety, national security, and community service.

A FORMER MILITARY OUTPOST

WHAT: St. Augustine houses the National Guard Armory and the National Guard in a building established in the 18th century.

WHERE: 82 Marine St.

COST: Free

PRO TIP: The St. Francis Barracks, a stop on the ACCORD Freedom Trail, is on the National Guard grounds along with a small museum of military history.

According to a guest book, the chapel of St. Francis Barracks is the source of paranormal experiences. Visitors report strange noises, cold spots, the sound of footsteps, and the appearance of apparitions.

ST. AUGUSTINE PIRATE & TREASURE MUSEUM

Why does this museum look so familiar?

This exhibit used to be known as the Pirate Soul Museum in Key West, but Pat Croce, former team president of the Philadelphia 76ers, bought it and moved it to St. Augustine in 2010. Croce contributed items from his own personal collection, and since then, the museum has expanded to become the largest assemblage of pirate relics and history in Florida.

There are almost 1,000 pirate items and 48 interactive exhibits. Authentic pirate memorabilia includes a treasure chest, a Jolly Roger flag, and the log of Captain Kidd. For added fun, visitors can feel the heft of a real gold brick. Designed to simulate a real pirate ship, visitors can man the helm to set sail with employees in the guise of pirates such as Anne Bonny, Mary Read, Blackbeard, Calico Jack Rackham, and other wanton privateers.

The museum sells tickets to the Black Raven, a pirate ship located at

A MUSEUM DEVOTED TO PIRATE LEGACIES

WHAT: Authentic pirate history and swag

WHERE: 12 S Castillo Dr.

COST: $17.99 for adults, $15.99 for children ages; 5–12; free for seniors, military, St. Johns residents, and children under five.

PRO TIP: Employees dress as pirates and adopt pirate names such as Anne Bonny.

The largest collection of pirate swag is attributed to the Whydah Pirate Museum in West Yarmouth, Massachusetts.

Top: *Life-size display of pirates conducting business at St. Augustine Pirate & Treasure Museum.* Inset: *A gruesome reenactment of Blackbeard's fate at the Pirate & Treasure Museum in St. Augustine.*

the St. Augustine Municipal Marina. It is usually packed with tourists chanting pirate ditties, replete with pirate jokes and knowledge of pirate swordplay and espionage. Many of the passengers are dressed as pirates. You can see them walking along the seawall to the marina, a reminder of the ruffians of yore.

CLASSIC CAR MUSEUM OF ST. AUGUSTINE

What do you do with more than 100 classic cars?

In the parking lot of the Classic Car Museum of St. Augustine is a yellow amphibious vehicle designed to drive on land and water. Inside the building is an art museum for cars featuring 30,000 square feet with more than 100 cars of every model, age, series, and quirky distinction. Even if you are not a "car person," the classic car museum is a must-see stop on a visit to St. Augustine. This is an art museum for cars. Included is a 1961 red Corvette that local businessman Sidney Hobbs spent a decade restoring.

In the process, he learned a lot about antique and classic cars and the collectors who owned them. After retiring from the medical supply business, Sidney, his wife, and ultimately his daughter founded the museum. He owns all but about 35 of the cars. There are fire trucks and ambulances, a 1969 Dodge Daytona, a Shelby Cobra Mustang, and Fords, Cadillacs, and Corvettes of every year and model. All the vehicles are classic or antique and in mint condition. The lobby also includes antique car

ANTIQUE AND CLASSIC CARS

WHAT: A museum of more than 100 classic cars

WHERE: 4730 US 1 S

COST: $15 for adults

PRO TIP: The 1895 Rochet-Schneider Roadster uses a bicycle chain to get power to its rear axle.

Florida is known for its classic car collector community; a private collector in Orlando owns more than 1,000.

The Classic Car Museum of St. Augustine began as a private collection. The museum even features a real Batmobile.

parts, gas pumps, and an 1895 Rochet-Schneider Roadster. The cars are rotated so each visit can yield unseen models on display.

The museum serves as a venue and regular meeting place for classic-car enthusiasts, and as a nonprofit; it hosts annual events for local high schools and charities like Toys for Tots and Safe Harbor Boys Academy.

It is open Tuesday through Saturday from 10 a.m. to 6 p.m.

HANG WITH A HAUNT AT HARRY'S SEAFOOD BAR & GRILLE

Who is the haunt in the women's bathroom at Harry's?

The line to get into Harry's usually snakes out to the sidewalk. There is outdoor seating with twinkle lights twined through the trees, downstairs dining, upstairs dining, and a bar. Why do people wait? Two reasons: the food and the secret in the women's bathroom.

First, the food: this is New Orleans cuisine, and Harry's knows how to do it. The red beans and rice are good for simple fare and the shrimp étouffée for a classic dish. There's a great wine and cocktail list. Try the Big Easy with spiced rum, Southern Comfort, and banana liqueur, and *laissez les bon temps rouler!*

The secret story involves Catalina De Porres who owned the house in the 18th century. She was booted out of St. Augustine during the British occupation in 1763 with all the other Spaniards. When she

NEW ORLEANS CUISINE AND A SPANISH GHOST

WHAT: The haunt at Harry's Seafood Bar & Grille lurks in the women's bathroom.

WHERE: 46 Avenida Menéndez

COST: Average cost of dishes ranges from $12 to $28.

PRO TIP: Catalina De Porres emigrated to Cuba with most of the other Spaniards in St. Augustine when the Treaty of Paris gave the territory to England.

Customers claim to have seen not only the ethereal Catalina but also a ghostly bride in white and a tall, transparent man wearing a frock coat.

An entrance to Harry's Seafood Bar & Grille in St. Augustine. The former Spanish owner of the original building is rumored to haunt the women's restroom at Harry's.

returned in 1783 during the second Spanish occupation, she reasserted ownership of her home. Alas, almost 100 years later, the St. Augustine fire of 1887 reduced the De Porres abode to ashes. Harry's was built to replicate the original, but maybe a little too closely. Legend has it that Catalina, a proper Spanish lady, hated the use of foul language. The upstairs women's bathroom is approximately close to Catalina's former bedroom. Local lore has it that if you curse in the bathroom, Catalina materializes to give you a good slap.

O. C. WHITE'S RESTAURANT: SEAFOOD & SPIRITS

What does the O. C. stand for in the restaurant's name?

Abutting Matanzas Bay, O. C. White's Restaurant has excellent seafood, which you can eat inside the 240-year-old building or outside in a fenced-in courtyard serenaded by live music. Over the centuries, its ownership has been eminent, including a royal treasurer, the widow of a general, the owner of the first cigar factory in St. Augustine, and the owner of a wax museum.

Presently, the historic site is owned by David and Cathy White, who purchased the coquina, wood, and steel building in 1990. The restaurant was restored to maintain its somewhat Victorian appearance in the 19th century, and 19th century issues continue to plague the restaurant.

Servers report flying glasses, dancing salt and pepper shakers, and mysterious footsteps. Some guests and employees claim to smell smoke around the anniversary date of a second-floor fire in 1992 whose source was never discovered. Stacked chairs were found the next day atop the tables.

It appears the Whites engaged in a double entendre when they named their popular restaurant. The seafood is fresh and superbly cooked. The spirits are plentiful and engaging, especially the St. Augustine Berry Lemonade. But drinks aren't the only spirits the Whites had in mind. There is a narrative on the menu about the

---

George Potter, owner of Potter's Wax Museum, had the house moved to its present location. It used to reside on Marine Street where the parking lot is today.

150

A view through the outdoor patio of O. C. White's

restaurant's ghostly and ongoing antics. So, it is no surprise that the restaurant's real name is Out-of-Control White's Seafood and Spirits.

The restaurant is located in the St. Augustine Town Plan Historic District, which is a National Historic Landmark District.

FRESH SEAFOOD AND A GHOSTLY HISTORY

WHAT: One of the best restaurants in St. Augustine with a ghostly history

WHERE: 118 Avenida Menéndez

COST: Averages $30–$50 a person

PRO TIP: The balcony on the second floor is a great place to watch Nights of Lights November through January.

FILL UP AT OBI'S FILLIN' STATION

Where is gas still advertised at pennies per gallon?

There are only seven car-themed restaurants in the United States, and Obi's Fillin' Station is one of them. Two old-fashioned gas pumps stand like sentries outside the restaurant, their price set at 26 cents. The interior is supposed to look like a garage. The bathroom sinks are mounted on transmissions, and guests sit on actual car seats. Eddie Obi Jr. and partner Angelo Hernandez opened the joint in 2015. Obi Jr. owns a car-related business in Jacksonville. His father owned a real filling station.

This is a small, casual place with a menu named after car parts like the Spare Tire, the Jaguar, and the Peugeot. Salads are Hybrids, and Crank Shafts are sides. The Finish Line features straightforward desserts like banana pudding, pie, and ice cream. This is simple American fare. Think burgers, meatball subs, fries, and melts. There are vegan entrées, and it serves breakfast, too, which many patrons praise.

A RESTAURANT FOR CAR LOVERS

WHAT: Obi's Fillin' Station, a car-themed restaurant

WHERE: 590 A1A Beach Blvd.

COST: $10–$18

PRO TIP: Tripadvisor ranks Obi's as No. 15 out of 116 restaurants on St. Augustine Beach.

Customers rave about Obi's iced coffee and lemonade.

Old-time gas pumps are among the decor at Obi's Fillin' Station. Obi is the last name of the original owner.

There is Happy Hour on Thursdays with craft beer, cocktails, and wine, and Obi's is open seven days a week from 8 a.m. to 7:45 p.m. Stop in on your way to St. Augustine Beach. If you ride your bike, there's an air pump outside the restaurant for tires.

HISPANIC PLAZA

What is another name for the Hispanic Plaza?

Located on the corner of Hypolita and St. George Street, the Hispanic Plaza is owned by the St. Augustine Foundation, and it's closed most of the time. It was closed to the public around 2001 when St. Augustine was cracking down on street theater and displays of art. Musicians and artists protested around the site, which resulted in its permanent closure except for special events (like the knighting of notable St. Augustine citizens). Still, there is a lot to see of the garden peering through the wrought iron fencing.

Dedicated in 1965 to commemorate the city's 400th anniversary, the project was planned and implemented by the Historic St. Augustine Preservation Board. The plaza, originally called Hispanic Garden, was created to imitate Spanish gardens found in colonial St. Augustine and Spain. A bronze statue in the center of the garden features Queen Isabella on a mule. Known as the "Catholic Monarch," she was queen of Castile and Aragon. Her

The Queen Isabella statue was removed for three years around the turn of the 21st century while archaeologists excavated the property. They found remnants of Spanish, British, and American occupation. The statue was replaced, but the iron fencing remains.

Spanish Queen Isabella and her footman at Hispanic Plaza

A SPANISH QUEEN IN A SPANISH GARDEN

WHAT: A beautiful Spanish garden in the center of St. Augustine, containing a statue of the 15th-century Queen of Spain

WHERE: Corner of Hypolita and St. George Streets

COST: Free

PRO TIP: The plaza has a trapezoid shape and pebbled grounds because there was no grass in Spanish gardens.

marriage to Ferdinand II unified Spain and funded the expeditions of Christopher Columbus.

It is notable that Queen Isabella was chosen to oversee the Spanish garden. Women championed the project, raised funds for it, and chose who would represent it. The statue was sculpted by Anna Hyatt Huntington, a member of the National Academy of Design and the National Sculpture Society. She also sculpted a statue of Joan of Arc erected in New York City.

The Queen Isabella statue is so popular in St. Augustine that the Hispanic Plaza is often referred to as Queen Isabella Garden.

PENNY MACHINES IN ST. AUGUSTINE

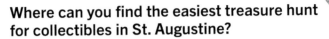

Where can you find the easiest treasure hunt for collectibles in St. Augustine?

Penny presses make great inexpensive souvenirs, and the machines are fun to hunt for children and adults. The presses elongate pennies into an oval shape by turning a crank. Then they print a design on the surface, usually including the city, store, or tourist location. The cost is around 50 cents for one penny.

Penny press machines date back to 1818 with an Austrian jeweler and gained popularity in the US at the end of the 19th century at the Chicago World's Fair. In those days, the coins were pressed on rollers. The first coin-operated penny press appeared in the 1970s, and every bicentennial has seen a resurgence in their popularity primarily for commemorative collectibles.

The process is simple. Locate a penny press machine (see the list below). Pick your design, and insert the quarters and penny into a slot on the machine. Watch as the machine flattens and embosses the coin. Once the coin is released, you'll have an instant souvenir to remember St. Augustine.

START A HOLIDAY HOBBY

WHAT: Press machines in St. Augustine

WHERE: See adjacent list

COST: 51 cents to $1.01 per design

PRO TIP: You can pick up a penny booklet at the Fountain of Youth gift shop.

A commemorative coin at the Fort Matanzas gift shop has a misprint with the name of the fort misspelled.

There are websites to help locate penny press machines around Florida (see bibliography). You even can buy booklets to store your pennies, and they make great art projects for unique wall designs. Here's a list of the penny press machines you can find in St. Augustine:

- Buc-ee's: 200 World Commerce Pkwy.
- Castillo de San Marcos: 1 S Castillo Dr.
- Outside Bin: 39 Wine Bar in City Gate Plaza, corner of St. George and Orange Streets
- Flagler College (hidden beside a pillar outside the bookstore): 74 King St.
- Heritage Walk Shopping Village near the east entrance: 162 St. George St.
- Old Town Trolley Welcome Center: 27 San Marco Ave.
- Ponce de León Fountain of Youth: 11 Magnolia Ave.
- Potter's Wax Museum: 31 Orange St.
- Prehistoric Florida: 127 St. George St.
- Ripley's Believe It or Not!: 19 San Marco Ave. (near the intersection of State Road A1A and South Castillo Drive)
- St. Augustine Lighthouse: 81 Lighthouse Ave.
- St. Augustine Alligator Farm Zoological Park: 999 Anastasia Blvd.
- St. Augustine Aquarium: 2045 State Rd. 16
- St. George's Row Shops: 106 St. George St.
- The Old Jail: 167 San Marco Ave.
- The St. Augustine & St. Johns County Visitor Information Center: 10 S Castillo Dr.

Penny press machine at the St. George Street Mall

ST. PHOTIOS GREEK ORTHODOX NATIONAL SHRINE

Why is a national shrine smack-dab in the center of St. Augustine's tourist district?

The original worshippers on these grounds date to the 18th century. They were from all over the Mediterranean area: Greece, Italy, Spain, Corsica. They became known as Minorcans, as they all shared a Mediterranean origin and religion.

They were recruited by a Scotsman, Dr. Andrew Turnbill, who realized, along with some of his business associates, he could become extremely wealthy by developing Florida. The men looked for workers who could stand the Florida heat. Turnbill, familiar with the Mediterranean, recruited Minorcans to Florida. In 1768, he founded the colony of New Smyrna named for a Greek city.

More than a thousand Minorcan immigrants followed him. Things did not go well. No one knows for sure what Turnbill promised, but the displaced immigrants became his indentured servants. Living conditions were bad, food was scarce, and disease was rampant. Almost half of the new colony was dead by the end of the first year.

The colonists left on the New Smyrna Minorca outpost finally walked away, quite literally, from their servitude in 1777, traveling 75 miles to St. Augustine. They settled near where the shrine resides on St. George Street and worshipped there. Today, St. Augustine is home to around 35,000 Minorcans and is considered their largest American settlement.

The modest shrine is a memorial to the first Greek settlers in the New World. Close to the City Gate, its brochure labels the shrine as the "Jewel of St. George Street." It is also a museum, a chapel filled with Byzantine frescoes (religious icons painted directly on walls and domes), and a gift store. There are self-guided and educational

A Greek Orthodox shrine with roots in the Minorcan migration from New Smyrna.

A MINORCAN SHRINE

WHAT: An enclave where the refugees from New Smyrna worshipped

WHERE: 41 St. George St.

COST: Donations accepted

PRO TIP: A tradition called "Let's Light a Candle" fills the shrine with candles in memory of the first Greek immigrants.

tours. Restored in 1982, it's the only Greek National Shrine in the United States, right in the middle of the historic tourist district.

Open Sunday to Saturday from 10 a.m. to 5 p.m.

St. Photios the Great was Patriarch of Constantinople around AD 860 He promoted Orthodox Christianity through his mission work.

ADULTS ONLY AT THE LLAMA RESTAURANT

At what age are customers allowed to "eat, drink, discover" at the Llama Restaurant?

This is fine dining, so prepare your palate with some sparkling water before you dig into this Peruvian experience. Chef and owner Marcel Vizcarra combines family recipes with his Peruvian chef's training in Japanese and French cuisine.

To say the food is good or great or excellent seems redundant. Llama Restaurant won the St. Augustine 2022 Open Table Diner's Choice Award as one of the 100 best restaurants in the country. It is unique fare, impossible to replicate. Try the Yuca fritos, and you'll never go back to french fries. The ceviche lima is breathtaking, and the anticuchos (chargrilled beef heart skewers) could be a new form of religion.

The drinks are reminiscent of the eclectic cocktail choices at Brennan's in New Orleans with names like Flower Bomb, the Lima Mule, and the Chichamosa made with champagne, purple corn, pineapple, lime, and spices.

The Llama Restaurant is a best-kept secret among locals because of its benign white storefront entrance and modest outdoor sign illustrating the outline of a llama. There is no lobby or check-in, and

A UNIQUE GOURMET RESTAURANT

WHAT: The Llama Restaurant is almost like a private club.

WHERE: 415 Anastasia Blvd.

COST: Menu prices range from $6 to $29.

PRO TIP: Parking can be a challenge; arrive early enough to park on the street.

A symbol of perseverance, llamas are extremely tall, growing as high as six feet.

the restaurant has only 28 tables. It requests reservations, and it's open every day except Monday from 5 to 8 p.m.

The restaurant prefers no children under the age of 8 darken the Llama's door as this is a serious epicurean experience.

An exclusive renowned restaurant on Anastasia Island, the Llama Restaurant requires reservations and no children allowed under the age of 8.

THE WITTY WHISKER CAT CAFE

What is a witty cat's favorite joke?

Since the 1990s when the first cat café opened in Taiwan, cat lovers have headed to local shops where they can buy food and drink in proximity to felines. In St. Augustine, that's the Witty Whisker Cat Cafe. The café is handy for people who adore cats but can't own one, whether because of a partner with allergies or an unyielding landlord. It's also great for someone looking for a pet as all of the furry inhabitants of the café are adoptable (individual cats are featured on the website). The Witty Whisker takes cats from kill shelters or people who need to find theirs a new home, as well as strays found on the street. The cats are petted and spoiled in a play area featuring a picture window, cat condos, a cat mansion, basket of toys and a big cat treadmill.

Why are the cats in this café witty? It's true cats are funny; they like to sleep in your slippers, climb on top of the refrigerator, and inherit all your money. But witty? I asked the owner, Angeli Rodriguez, who wrote a book titled *Drinks & Whiskers: How You Can Open a Successful Cat Cafe*, why she chose the name. She said, "No reason. I just liked the alliteration."

Still, I read some jokes aloud to Stella, a nine-year-old tabby. She purred the loudest for this one:

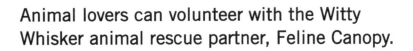

> **Why did the cat wear a fancy dress?**
> *She was feline fine.*

Animal lovers can volunteer with the Witty Whisker animal rescue partner, Feline Canopy.

FOR CAT LOVERS

WHAT: Meet witty cats who are feline fine

WHERE: 112 N Ponce de León Blvd.

COST: $11 fee to access the cat lounge

PRO TIP: The Witty Whisker Cat Cafe accepts reservations and appointments for special events.

Top: *An exterior shot of the Witty Whisker Cat Cafe on Ponce de León Boulevard.*
Inset: *A feline patron gets a workout at the Witty Whisker Cat Café.*

The café serves witty coffee drinks, breakfast sandwiches, and desserts. Located near Flagler College, The Witty Whisker is open six days a week until 6 p.m. on weekdays and 8 p.m. on weekends. Closed on Tuesday.

ST. AUGUSTINE AQUARIUM

What friendly vertebrate swims to greet staff?

Owners Shawn and Kathy Hiester originally planned to open on Riberia Street in 2016, but instead chose to open on State Road 16 for the increased acreage, parking advantages, and traffic exposure. The aquarium is a nonprofit outdoor facility focused on human–maritime interaction and education. In Stingray Cove, the rays actually recognize staff and bob up for petting. Elsewhere, seahorses hide in sawgrass. There's a hands-on touch habitat where you can touch starfish, horseshoe crabs, and other invertebrates. You can feed the fish as well.

Funded by a variety of corporate sponsors and an Adopt an Animal program, the aquarium offers guided tours led by marine biologists, as well as snorkeling in an 80,000-gallon tank with friendly reef fish and rays. The aquarium supplies the wetsuits, masks, and snorkels. Celebrations, birthday parties, and events are often held at the open-air facility.

Originally from Pennsylvania, the Heisters combine their love for outdoor adventure with providing a safe maritime experience for the creatures in their care. They quit their jobs and studied

INTERACT WITH SEA LIFE

WHAT: An outdoor marine attraction on State Road 16

WHERE: 2045 State Rd. 16

COST: $12.95 for adults, $8.95 for children

PRO TIP: A zip line used to be an accommodation, but it wasn't in service during a recent visit.

A new adventure is planned for the future where divers can be lowered in a cage to an artificial reef, shipwreck, and live sharks.

Visitors and staff hand-feed and pet rays at the St. Augustine Aquarium.

marine biology to provide this facility for St. Johns and Duval County residents. Many of the groupers, grunts, sharks, and rays are survivors of injuries who otherwise would not last long in the surrounding waters of the briny deep.

The St. Augustine Aquarium is open Monday through Friday from 9 a.m. to 4 p.m. and Saturday and Sunday from 9 a.m. to 5 p.m.

NIGHTS OF LIGHTS IN ST. AUGUSTINE

What is the origin of the Nights of Lights in St. Augustine?

St. Augustine is the oldest continuously occupied city in America, swapping allegiances from the Spanish to the British and back to the Spanish again. Although the United States took possession of the territory in 1821, its European and predominantly Spanish influence remains strong well into the 21st century. The Nights of Lights is an example.

Based on the tradition of putting white candles in the windows of Spanish casas during the winter holidays, the city of St. Augustine celebrates Christmas from November 18 through January 31 with a glorious display of white lights that envelope the roofs, trees, monuments, and buildings of the entire historic district.

The tradition of the beautiful St. Augustine festival began in the 1990s when two businessmen observed a similar sight in Tennessee. When they returned home, they began fundraising and eventually entered into a collaboration with the city, the Tourist Development Council, and area businesses.

A FAMOUS ST. AUGUSTINE TRADITION

WHAT: A Christmas display of lights enveloping the entire city

WHERE: The shuttle meets at 10 Castillo Dr. behind the Visitor Information Center

COST: A trolley tour or a cruise to observe the lights is about $40.

PRO TIP: Over three million lights are used in the Nights of Lights display.

National Geographic cited Nights of Lights as one of the best Christmas light exhibits on the globe.

Top: *A night view of the City Gate and St. George Street during St. Augustine's Nights of Lights.* Inset: *Ponce de León points north during the Nights of Lights, December 18 through January 31 in St. Augustine.*

An architectural firm designs the lighting displays and installs them every year. Enjoying the lights is free, and there are numerous tours throughout the season to view the holiday exhibit: by trolley, boat, or air; from the lighthouse; from the Bridge of Lions; or from any of the restaurant or hotel balconies. The holiday sight draws thousands of tourists every year.

OLD TOWN TROLLEY TOURS

Which one of the Old Town Trolley Tour founders had a father who took an iconic picture for a famous newspaper?

In the 1970s, best buddies Chris Belland, Mo Mosher, and Ed Swift started the trolley tours in Key West using an old bread wagon with a trailer on the back. In 1980, they formed a partnership called Historic Tours of America, which quickly went national in San Diego; Boston; Washington, DC; Savannah; and St. Augustine. Headquarters are still in Key West where Belland, Wharton School of Business graduate and lifelong Conch, is CEO.

Old Town Trolley Tours are a lot cheaper than a horse-drawn carriage and a little cheaper than Red Train Tours. They have 21 stops; you can hop on and off at any of them. The website lists every stop with information and displays of other attractions nearby.

The tour is about 90 minutes if you stay on, but you can extend it if you want to explore an area and continue the trolley tour later. Some attractions are free with a trolley

THE BEST WAY TO SEE ST. AUGUSTINE

WHAT: A trolley tour to see the sights of St. Augustine at your own pace

WHERE: 167 San Marco Ave.

COST: $36.55 for adults, $17.77 for kids ages 4–12

PRO TIP: Ed Swift, one of the founders of Historic Tours of America, owned a camera shop in Key West for many years. His father was the photographer for the *St. Louis Star-Times* who took the picture of President Truman holding up the newspaper with the headline "DEWEY DEFEATS TRUMAN."

Voted "Best Guided Tour by Best in St. Augustine 2023

The Old Town Trolley in St. Augustine is a solution to the lack of parking in the ancient city.

ticket: Gator Bob's Old St. Augustine History Museum, St. Augustine Alligator Farm Zoological Park, and the beach shuttle. The trolley even picks you up and drops you off at some hotels. You can find positive reviews on Yelp, and some tourists buy tickets just to avoid parking issues.

Avenida Menéndez Seawall

SOURCES

The author and photographer personally visited each site more than once.

Mission Nombre de Dios Museum:
Edwards, Virginia. *Stories of Old St. Augustine.* Paramount Press, Jacksonville, Florida, 1971; Graham, Thomas. *The Awakening of St. Augustine.* St. Augustine Historical Society, 1978; J.T. Campen, *St. Augustine, Florida's Colonial Capital,* St. Augustine Historical Society, 1959; Mission Nombre de Dios Museum, Swarb, Amy. "Florida celebrates 500th anniversary but history blurred by myth," Reuters, 2013.

Old Spanish Quarries: Adams, William R. *St. Augustine and St. Johns County: A Historical Guide.* Pineapple Press Inc., 2009; Edwards, Virginia. *Stories of Old St. Augustine.* Paramount Press, Jacksonville, Florida, 1971; Hall, Maggi Smith. *St. Augustine.* Arcadia Publishing, 2002.

City Gate: Arnade, Charles. *The Siege of St. Augustine.* UF Monograph, 1959; Edwards, Virginia. *Stories of Old St. Augustine.* Paramount Press, Jacksonville, Florida, 1971; J.T. Campen, *St. Augustine, Florida's Colonial Capital,* St. Augustine Historical Society, 1959.

Plaza de la Constitución: Adams, William R. *St. Augustine and St. Johns County: A Historical Guide,* Pineapple Press, Sarasota, Florida, 2009; Edwards, Virginia. *Stories of Old St. Augustine.* Paramount Press, Jacksonville, Florida, 1971; Graham, Thomas. *The Awakening of St. Augustine.* St. Augustine Historical Society, 1978; Graham, Thomas. *Mr. Flagler's St. Augustine.* UF Press, Florida, 2014; J.T. Campen, *St. Augustine, Florida's Colonial Capital,* St. Augustine Historical Society, 1959.

Historic Public Market at the Plaza de la Constitución: Adams, William R. *St. Augustine and St. Johns County: A Historical Guide,* Pineapple Press, Sarasota, Florida, 2009; J.T. Campen, *St. Augustine, Florida's Colonial Capital,* St. Augustine Historical Society, 1959; Goldstein, Holly. "St. Augustine's Slave Market: A Visual History," *Brewminate,* 2021; Pope, Margo. "Slavery and the Oldest City," *The St. Augustine Record,* December 2, 2001.

St. George Street: Edwards, Virginia. *Stories of Old St. Augustine.* Paramount Press, Jacksonville, Florida, 1971; J.T. Campen, *St. Augustine, Florida's Colonial Capital,* St. Augustine Historical Society, 1959. Reynolds, Charles Bingham. *The Standard Guide, St. Augustine.* EH Reynolds, 1890.

Old Spanish Well and Chimney: Adams, William R. *St. Augustine and St. Johns County: A Historical Guide.* Pineapple Press Inc., 2009; Edwards, Virginia. *Stories of Old St. Augustine.* Paramount Press, Jacksonville, Florida, 1971; J.T. Campen, *St. Augustine, Florida's Colonial Capital,* St. Augustine Historical Society, 1959.

Mayport
Authority, Port. "Brochure: The Buccaneer Trail, Florida A1A Avoid City Congestion Travel Florida's New

Seashore Route–Along the East Coast."
(1958); Wilson, Rex L. *Excavations at
the Mayport Mound, Florida*. No. 13.
University of Florida, 1965; Lepore,
Brian J., Mark J. Wielgoszynski, Pat L.
Bohan, Susan Ditto, Brandon Jones,
Carol Petersen, Michael Shaughnessy,
and Government Accountability
Office, Washington, DC "Defense
Infrastructure: Navy's Analysis of Costs
and Benefits Regarding Naval Station
Mayport Demonstrated Some Best
Practices and Minimally Addressed
Other Requirements." (2013).

Fort Mose Historic State Park:
Arnade, Charles. *The Siege of St.
Augustine.* UF Monograph, 1959;
J.T. Campen, *St. Augustine, Florida's
Colonial Capital,* St. Augustine
Historical Society, 1959; Edwards,
Virginia. *Stories of Old St. Augustine.*
Paramount Press, Jacksonville, Florida,
1971; Fort Mose, Historic State Park,
Fort Mose Historic State Park | Florida
State Parks; Landers, Jane L. *Black
Society in Spanish St. Augustine,
1784–1821*. University of Florida,
1988; Landers, Jane, "Spanish
Sanctuary: Fugitives in Florida, 1687–
1790," Florida Historical Quarterly 62,
No. 3, 1984.

Spanish Military Hospital Museum:
Edwards, Virginia. *Stories of Old
St. Augustine.* Paramount Press,
Jacksonville, Florida, 1971; J.T.
Campen, *St. Augustine, Florida's
Colonial Capital,* St. Augustine
Historical Society, 1959; Spanish
Military Hospital Museum,
Spanish Military Hospital Museum
(smhmuseum.com); Storrs,
Christopher. "Health, Sickness and
Medical Services in Spain's Armed
Forces c. 1665–1700." *Medical
History* 50, No. 3 (2006): 325–350.

**Fourth of July at Castillo de San
Marcos:** Arnade, Charles. *The Siege
of St. Augustine.* UF Monograph,
1959; Edwards, Virginia. *Stories of
Old St. Augustine.* Paramount Press,
Jacksonville, Florida, 1971; J.T.
Campen, *St. Augustine, Florida's
Colonial Capital,* St. Augustine
Historical Society, 1959.

Colonial Oak Music Park: Colonial Oak
Music Park Live Music in the Heart of
the Historic District | St. Augustine &
Ponte Vedra, FL (floridashistoriccoast.
com); Colonial Oak Music Park, The
Colonial Oak Music Park – The Colonial
Oak Music Park.

Huguenot Cemetery: Coquina
Crosses at the Huguenot Cemetery,
"Huguenot Cemetery." *Florida Division
of Historical Resources,* Florida
Department of State, 2023, Huguenot
Cemetery - Division of Historical
Resources - Florida Department of
State.

**Governor's House Cultural Center
and Museum:** Barnewolt, Claire M.
"'Let the Castillo be his Monument!'
Imperialism, Nationalism, and Indian
Commemoration at the Castillo de
San Marcos National Monument in St.
Augustine, Florida." (2018); Gardner,
Sheldon. "A beautiful history: St.
Augustine exhibit includes paintings
of bygone city life," *St. Augustine
Record,* May 2022.

**Constitution Obelisk in the Plaza de
la Constitución:** Cosme, Raphael.
"The Real History of the Obelisk in St.
Augustine's Plaza de la Constitución,"
Historic City News, April 19, 2012;
Edwards, Virginia. *Stories of Old
St. Augustine.* Paramount Press,
Jacksonville, Florida, 1971; J.T.
Campen, *St. Augustine, Florida's
Colonial Capital,* St. Augustine

Historical Society, 1959; Mirow, M.C. "Translating into Stone: The Monument to the Constitution of Cadiz in Saint Augustine, Florida." In: Hook, D., Iglesias-Rogers, G. (eds) Translations In Times of Disruption. Palgrave Studies in Translating and Interpreting. Palgrave Macmillan, London, 2017.

Cannon Fire in St. Augustine: Cannons at the Castillo De San Marcos, Castillo de San Marcos National Monument (US National Park Service) (nps.gov).

Avenida Menéndez Seawall: Bowen, Beth Rogero. *St. Augustine in the Gilded Age*. Arcadia Publishing, 2008. Nolan, David. *The Houses of St. Augustine*. Pineapple Press Inc., 1995; Parker, Susan. "Nation's Oldest City: Seawall keeps the ocean out of St. Augustine," *St. Augustine Record*, February 11, 2011.

Fountain of Youth Archaeological Park: Brotemarkle, Benjamin D. "The Florida Historical Society Presents an Original Courtroom Drama: Ponce de León Landed HERE!!" *The Florida Historical Quarterly* 92.1 (2013): 106–127; Edwards, Virginia. *Stories of Old St. Augustine*. Paramount Press, Jacksonville, Florida, 1971; "Fountain of Youth Park Water," *All-American Adventure Guide*, Fountain of Youth Park Water - All-American Adventure Guide (allamericanadventureguide. com).

Fort Matanzas National Park: Dorr, Jessica, David Palmer, Rebecca Schneider, John M. Galbraith, Myles Killar, Scott D.; Fort Matanzas National Park, Fort Matanzas National Monument (US National Park Service) (nps.gov); Klopfer, Linsey C. Marr, and Eric Wolf. "Natural Resource Condition Assessment: Castillo de San Marcos and Fort Matanzas National Monuments, Florida." (2012); Gardner, Sheldon. "Fort Matanzas in St. Johns County reopens to visitors following Covid closure," *St. Augustine Record*, July 21, 2021.

Oldest House Museum Complex: Tingley, Charles. *St. Augustine Historical Society,* Fire Hat at Oldest House, 21 Nov. 2023; González-Alvarez House, Oldest House Museum I Visit St. Augustine (visitstaugustine. com); Stephensen, John. *González-Alvarez House*, phone interview, October 7, 2023.

Oldest Wooden Schoolhouse Historic Museum & Gardens: Edwards, Virginia. *Stories of Old St. Augustine*. Paramount Press, Jacksonville, Florida, 1971; "Greeks remember founder of oldest wooden schoolhouse," *St. Augustine Record*, March 5, 2020.

Horruytiner/Lindsley House: Edwards, Virginia. *Stories of Old St. Augustine*. Paramount Press, Jacksonville, Florida, 1971; Harvey, Karen. *Oldest Ghosts: St. Augustine Haunts*. Pineapple Press Inc., 2000; Nolan, David. *The Houses of St. Augustine*. Pineapple Press Inc., 1995; Parker, Susan Richbourg. "St. Augustine in the Seventeenth-Century: Capital of La Florida." *The Florida Historical Quarterly* 92, No. 3 (2014): 554–576; Randall, Elizabeth. *Murder in St. Augustine: The Mysterious Death of Athalia Ponsell Lindsley*. Arcadia Publishing, 2016.

Ximenez-Fatio House Museum: Brotemarkle, Dr Ben. "Florida Frontiers TV–Episode 46–The Ximenez-Fatio House." (2021); Diffley, Kathleen. *Witness to Reconstruction: Constance Fenimore Woolson and the Postbellum South, 1873–1894*. Univ. Press of Mississippi, 2011; Grissino-Mayer, Henri D., Leda N. Kobziar, Grant L. Harley, Kevin P.

Russell, Lisa B. LaForest, and Joseph K. Oppermann. "The historical dendroarchaeology of the Ximenez-Fatio House, St. Augustine, Florida, USA." *Tree-Ring Research* 66, No. 1 (2010): 61–73; Woolson, Constance Fenimore. *Constance Fenimore Woolson: Selected Stories and Travel Narratives.* Univ. of Tennessee Press, 2004.

Peña-Peck House Museum: Brooke, Steven. *The Majesty of St. Augustine.* Pelican Publishing, 2005; Sander, Kathleen Waters. *The business of charity: The woman's exchange movement, 1832–1900.* Vol. 159. University of Illinois Press, 1998; The Women's Exchange of St. Augustine, https://penapeckhouse.com

Casa Monica Resort & Spa: Ayers, Wayne. *Florida's grand hotels from the Gilded Age,* Arcadia Publishing, Charleston, SC,2005; Bowen, Beth. *St. Augustine in the Gilded Age,* Arcadia Puslave market publishing, Charleston, SC, 2008; Edwards, Virginia. *Stories of Old St. Augustine.* Paramount Press, Jacksonville, Florida, 1971; Graham, Thomas. *The Awakening of St. Augustine.* St. Augustine Historical Society, 1978; Graham, Thomas. *Mr. Flagler's St. Augustine.* UF Press, Florida, 2014.

Ponce de León Statues: Brotemarkle, Benjamin D. "The Florida Historical Society Presents an Original Courtroom Drama: Ponce de León Landed HERE!!." *The Florida Historical Quarterly* 92.1 (2013): 106–127; Graham, Thomas. *The Awakening of St. Augustine.* St. Augustine Historical Society, 1978; Graham, Thomas. *Mr. Flagler's St. Augustine.* UF Press, Florida, 2014; GTM Research Reserve Research Center, GTM Research Reserve Visitor Center

| St. Augustine & Ponte Vedra, FL (floridashistoriccoast.com).

Pyramids at St. Augustine National Cemetery: Dade Pyramids, St. Augustine Florida, Dade Pyramids at St. Augustine National Cemetery - Florida (exploresouthernhistory.com).

Moultrie Church and Wildwood Cemetery: Adams, William R. *St. Augustine and St. Johns County: A Historical Guide.* Pineapple Press Inc., 2009; Harris, Jason Marc. "Shadows of the Past in the Sunshine State: St. Augustine Ghost Lore and Tourism." *Western Folklore* (2015): 309–342; McKoy, Kimeko. "Where History Lives: Years of history at Moultrie Church, Wildwood Cemetery," *The St. Augustine Record,* December 7, 2014; Siebert, Wilbur H. "Slavery and white servitude in East Florida, 1726 to 1776." *The Florida Historical Society Quarterly* 10, No. 1 (1931): 3–23.

St. Augustine Lighthouse & Maritime Museum: Dillon, Doug. *St. Augustine.* Mitchell Lane Publishers Inc., 2010; Fleming, Kathy. "St. Augustine Lighthouse and Fresnel Lens," *Visit Florida,* accessed Oct. 2023; St. Augustine Lighthouse, staugustinelighthouse.org.

Lightner Museum: Bowen, Beth. *St. Augustine in the Gilded Age,* Arcadia Puslave market publishing, Charleston, SC, 2008; Gravestone of O. C. Lightner at Lightner Museum, https://www.floridamemory.com/items/show/78138.

The Sundial at Flagler College: Ayers, Wayne. *Florida's grand hotels from the Gilded Age,* Arcadia Publishing, Charleston, SC, 2005; Bowen, Beth. *St. Augustine in the Gilded Age,* Arcadia Puslave market publishing, Charleston, SC, 2008; Edwards,

Virginia. *Stories of Old St. Augustine.* Paramount Press, Jacksonville, Florida, 1971; Historic Tours of Flagler College, Historic Tours of Flagler College - Flagler's Legacy.

Bridge of Lions: Bridge of Lions, Bridge of Lions I St. Augustine, FL (citystaug.com); Lane, Marcia. "Bridge Opening Remembered." *St. Augustine Record,* March 17, 2010; Brook, Steve. "The Majesty of St. Augustine," Pelican Publishing, Gretna, Louisiana, 2005; Edwards, Virginia. *Stories of Old St. Augustine.* Paramount Press, Jacksonville, Florida, 1971.

Flagler Memorial Presbyterian Church: Brook, Steve. "The Majesty of St. Augustine," Pelican Publishing, Gretna, Louisiana, 2005; Gardner, Sheldon. "Flagler's church one of '8 religious wonders,' CNN says," *St. Augustine Record,* July 10, 2012; Graham, Thomas. *The Awakening of St. Augustine.* St. Augustine Historical Society, 1978; Graham, Thomas. *Mr. Flagler's St. Augustine.* UF Press, Florida, 2014.

Zora Neale Hurston House: Clark, Jessica. "Author Zora Neale Hurston's St. Augustine home is for sale," *First Coast News,* Jan. 2023; Randall, Elizabeth. *An Ocklawaha River Odyssey: Paddling through Natural History.* Arcadia Publishing, 2019; Zora Neale Hurston, Zora Neale Hurston I Visit St. Augustine (visitstaugustine.com). Randall, Elizabeth. "Save the Zora Neale Hurston House in St. Augustine," Substack, July, 2023.

Lincolnville Museum and Cultural Center: Lincolnville Museum and Cultural Center, www. lincolnvillemuseum.org; Slate, Claudia S. "Florida Room: Battle for St. Augustine 1964: Public Record and Personal Recollection," Florida Historical Quarterly: Vol. 84: No. 4, Article 5. 2005; Smith, Chloe, "Corner Market mural to bring African American history back to life in St. Augustine," Flagler College Gargoyle, February 20, 2023.

The Windows of Flagler College: Ayers, Wayne. *Florida's grand hotels from the Gilded Age,* Arcadia Publishing, Charleston, SC, 2005; Field Trip: Antiques Roadshow Flagler College, Field Trip: Flagler Tiffany Windows I Antiques Roadshow I PBS; Graham, Thomas. "Flagler's Magnificent Hotel Ponce de León." *The Florida Historical Quarterly* 54, No. 1 (1975): 1–17; Keys, Leslee F. *Hotel Ponce de León: The Rise, Fall, and Rebirth of Flagler's Gilded Age Palace.* University Press of Florida, 2018.

Villa Zorayda Museum: Ayers, Wayne. *Florida's grand hotels from the Gilded Age,* Arcadia Publishing, Charleston, SC, 2005; Bowen, Beth. *St Augustine in the Gilded Age,* Arcadia Puslave market publishing, Charleston, SC, 2008; Edwards, Virginia. *Stories of Old St. Augustine.* Paramount Press, Jacksonville, Florida, 1971; Graham, Thomas. *The Awakening of St. Augustine.* St. Augustine Historical Society, 1978; Graham, Thomas. *Mr. Flagler's St. Augustine.* UF Press, Florida, 2014; Harvey, Karen. *America's First City,* Tailored Tours Pub, Florida, 1997; Villa Zyola Museum, www.villazorayda.com.

Corner Market: Lincolnville Museum and Cultural Center, www. lincolnvillemuseum.org; Phone Interview, Nyk Smith, Dec. 1, 2023. Paying the Price for Equal Rights in America's Oldest City, Explore St. Augustine's Civil Rights History – US Civil Rights Trail; Slate, Claudia S.

"Florida Room: Battle for St. Augustine 1964: Public Record and Personal Recollection," Florida Historical Quarterly: Vol. 84: No. 4, Article 5. 2005; Smith Chloe, "Corner Market mural to bring African American history back to life in St. Augustine," Flagler College Gargoyle, February 20, 2023.

Chill Out at the Ice Plant Bar: Ice Plant Bar Menu - Ice Plant Bar; Simons Jr., George W. "Saint Augustine, Florida: Comprehensive City Plan." (1960); Walking Through History Blog, St. Augustine's Ice Plant Historic Buildings Walking Tours (staugustinehistorictours.com).

Old St. Johns County Jail: Bowen, Beth Rogero. *St. Augustine in the Gilded Age.* Arcadia Publishing, 2008; Old Jail, Old Jail St. Augustine Information Guide (trolleytours.com); Slate, Claudia S. "Florida Room: Battle for St. Augustine 1964: Public Record and Personal Recollection." *The Florida Historical Quarterly* 84, No. 4 (2006): 541-568.

Manly Portable Convict Car: Manly Portable Convict Cage, The Historical Marker Data Base, Manly Portable Convict Cage Historical Marker (hmdb.org).

Gator Bob's Old St. Augustine History Museum: Gator Bob's Trading Post, Gator Bob's St. Augustine Information Guide (trolleytours.com).

Potter's Wax Museum: Potter's Wax Museum, www.potterswaxmuseum.com/; Torchia, Robert Wilson. Lost Colony: The Artists of St. Augustine, 1930–1950. Lightner Museum, 2001.

Bluebird of Happiness at Vilano Beach: "Around the Region, Happy Birthday to the Vilano Bluebird of Happiness." *St. Augustine Record,* June 4, 2015;

Bluebird of Happiness, Our History – Vilano Beach (vilanobeachfl.com); "Vilano's Bluebird is Coming Back," *St. Augustine Record*, Feb. 5, 2010.

Love Tree at the Bar Harbor Cheesecake Company: Growing Together: The Love Trees of St. Augustine, Growing Together: The Love Trees Of St. Augustine - Ripley's Believe It or Not! (ripleys.com); Love Tree, Love Tree, St. Augustine, Florida (roadsideamerica.com).

Dr. Robert B. Hayling Freedom Park: Paying the Price for Equal Rights in America's Oldest City, Explore St. Augustine's Civil Rights History – US Civil Rights Trail; Robert B. Hayling Freedom Park, Facilities • St. Augustine, FL • CivicEngage (citystaug.com); Slate, Claudia S. "Florida Room: Battle for St. Augustine 1964: Public Record and Personal Recollection," Florida Historical Quarterly: Vol. 84: No. 4, Article 5. 2005; Tis, Bob. "Let Freedom Ring at Hayley Park," *St. Augustine Record*, Jan. 2016.

Saint Paul AME Church: Gardner, Sheldon. "Historic St. Augustine church welcomes new leadership as 150th anniversary approaches," *St. Augustine Record,* January 28, 2022; Lincolnville Museum and Cultural Center, www.lincolnvillemuseum.org; Paying the Price for Equal Rights in America's Oldest City, Explore St. Augustine's Civil Rights History – US Civil Rights Trail; Slate, Claudia S. "Florida Room: Battle for St. Augustine 1964: Public Record and Personal Recollection," Florida Historical Quarterly: Vol. 84: No. 4, Article 5. 200; Smith Chloe, "Corner Market mural to bring African American history back to life in St. Augustine," Flagler College Gargoyle, February 20, 2023.

ACCORD Civil Rights Museum: Paying the Price for Equal Rights in America's Oldest City, Explore St. Augustine's Civil Rights History – US Civil Rights Trail; Slate, Claudia S. "Florida Room: Battle for St. Augustine 1964: Public Record and Personal Recollection," Florida Historical Quarterly: Vol. 84: No. 4, Article 5. 2005; Smith Chloe, "Corner Market mural to bring African American history back to life in St. Augustine," Flagler College Gargoyle, February 20, 2023.

ACCORD Freedom Trail: Paying the Price for Equal Rights in America's Oldest City, Explore St. Augustine's Civil Rights History – US Civil Rights Trail; Tis, Bob. "Let Freedom Ring at Hayley Park," *St. Augustine Record*, Jan. 2016.

MLK Jr.'s Steps at the Hilton Historic Bayfront Hotel: "Martin Luther King Jr Arrest Site - Hilton St. Augustine Historic Bayfront," Historic Coast Culture, accessed October 13, 2023; Paying the Price for Equal Rights in America's Oldest City, Explore St. Augustine's Civil Rights History – US Civil Rights Trail; Slate, Claudia S. "Florida Room: Battle for St. Augustine 1964: Public Record and Personal Recollection," Florida Historical Quarterly: Vol. 84: No. 4, Article 5. 2005; Smith Chloe, "Corner Market mural to bring African American history back to life in St. Augustine," Flagler College Gargoyle, February 20, 2023.

Athalia Ponsell Lindsley House on Marine Street: "Athalia Lindsley: The 42-year-old St Augustine who-done-it," *Historic City News,* January 23, 2016. Powell, Nancy. *Bloody Sunset in St. Augustine,* Federal Point Pub Inc., January 1, 1998; Randall, Elizabeth. Haunted St. Augustine and St. Johns County, the History Press, Mt. Pleasant, SC, 2011; Randall, Elizabeth. *Murder in St. Augustine,* History Press, 2016.

David at Ripley's Believe It or Not!: Jones, Colleen. "10 things you probably didn't know about Ripley's Believe It or Not! in St. Augustine," *St. Augustine Record,* Oct. 6, 2021; Ripley's Believe It or Not, www.ripleys.com/staugustine/

Southernmost Point Buoy Replica: PRI Productions, Props Rentals - PRI Productions

Schooner Freedom Charters: Miller, Mike. Florida Day Trips, Adventure Publications, Cambridge, Minnesota, 2020; Sail the *Schooner Freedom*, www.schoonerfreedom.com.

South-A-Philly Steaks & Hoagies: Greg and Mack Godzilla Pinball Review; (Stern) 2021, Bing Videos.

I Scream, You Scream for Mayday Handcrafted Ice Creams: Mayday Handcrafted Ice Creams, maydayicecream.com.

Pop into the Hyppo Gourmet Ice Pops Shop: The Hyppo Gourmet Ice Pops, thehyppo.com.

Micro Masterpieces Art Gallery: Micro Masterpieces Gallery in St. Augustine Florida, Abnormal Voyages, All The Small Things - (Micro Masterpieces Gallery in St. Augustine, Florida) - YouTube, accessed October 17, 2023.

Sarbez!: Personal interview with owner Ryan Kunsch, November 13, 2023. Sarbez!, www.sarbezstaug.com.

Convene at Cap's on the Water: Cap's on the Water, www.capsonthewater.com; Jones, Colleen. Which St. Augustine restaurant won a major award for its beautiful waterfront setting? *St. Augustine Record*, August 8, 2022.

Whetstone Chocolates' Original Chocolate Tour: Whetstone Chocolates Store and Tasting Tour, www.whetstonechocolates.com.

San Sebastian Winery: Bates, Robert. "The History of Grapes in Florida and Grape Pioneers," Institute of Food and Agricultural Sciences, University of Florida, Gainesville, 2013; San Sebastian Winery, Award Winning Florida Wines - San Sebastian Winery.

St. Augustine Beach Sculpture Garden: Guinta, Peter. "Sculpture Garden creator Thomas Glover W. dies." *St. Augustine Record*, May 20, 2012.

St. Augustine Alligator Farm Zoological Park: St. Augustine Alligator Farm Zoological Park: An Old Attraction with New Life I St. Augustine & Ponte Vedra, FL (floridashistoriccoast.com) St. Augustine Ponte Vedra, Florida's Historic Coast, Accessed November 8, 2023.

Bird Island Park: Bird Island Park, St. Johns County Government, St Johns County Bird Island Park (st-johns.fl.us); GTM Research Reserve Research Center, GTM Research Reserve Visitor Center I St. Augustine & Ponte Vedra, FL (floridashistoriccoast.com).

Weathervane at Howard Johnson Motor Lodge: Hoover, Gary. "The First Giant Restaurant Chain: Howard Johnson's: Rise and Fall," *American Business History Center,* August 26, 2021; Jones, Colleen, "More development slated for busy SR 16," *St. Augustine Record,* Dec. 28, 2018; Worth Point, HOWARD JOHNSON'S WEATHERVANE 1950's I #323781864 (worthpoint.com).

St. Augustine Surf Culture & History Museum: St. Augustine Surf Culture & History Museum, St. Augustine Surf Museum I St. Augustine & Ponte Vedra, FL (floridashistoriccoast.com).

Old Spanish Trail Zero Milestone Marker: https://www.nps.gov/nr/travel/american_latino_heritage/old_spanish_national_historic_trail.html; "Trail of Florida's Indian Heritage," CENTRAL - Trail of Florida's Indian Heritage (trailoffloridasindianheritage.org).

Ribera Garden: "Dedication Ceremonies Held for Ribera Garden." *St. Augustine Record,* May 5, 1968

Prohibition Kitchen: Kolmer, Elise. "Prohibition Kitchen pairs early 20th-century influence with modern trends," *St. Augustine Record*, October 18, 2018.

Florida National Guard Headquarters: "Centuries worth of history at St. Francis Barracks," *St. Augustine Record,* May 24, 2015; Florida department of Military Affairs, dma.myflorida.com.

St. Augustine Pirate & Treasure Museum: Konstam, Angus, and David Rickman. *Pirate: The Golden Age.* Bloomsbury Publishing, 2011; St. Augustine Pirate & Treasure Museum, www.thepiratemuseum.com.

Classic Car Museum of St. Augustine: Jones, Colleen, "More development slated for busy SR 16," *St. Augustine Record,* Dec. 28, 2018; Willott, Peter. "Classic Car Museum of St. Augustine boasts nearly 100 models and is an enthusiast's dream," *St. Augustine Record*, March 29, 2021.

Hang with a Haunt at Harry's Seafood Bar & Grille: Harry's Seafood Bar & Grille, hookedonharrys.com/location/st-augustine; Randall, Elizabeth. Haunted St. Augustine and St. Johns County, the History Press, Mt. Pleasant, SC, 2011.

O. C. White's Restaurant: Seafood & Spirits: Randall, Elizabeth. Haunted St. Augustine and St. Johns County, the History Press, Mt. Pleasant, SC, 2011.

Fill Up at Obi's Fillin' Station: Obi's Fillin' Station, www.obisfillin.com.

Hispanic Plaza: McCoy, Kameko. "Where History Lives: The Hispanic Garden offers a piece of Spain in St. Augustine," *St. Augustine Record*, June 7, 2021.

Penny Machines in St. Augustine: Penny Machines in St. Augustine, www.pennycollector.com; St. Augustine Florida Penny Presses, www.pennypresses.com; Where to find Penny Presses Across the US, Where to Find Pressed Penny Machines Across the U.S. - Our Roaming Hearts.

St. Photios Greek Orthodox National Shrine: Griffin, Patricia. Mullet on the Beach: The Minorcans of Florida, 1768–1788, Library Press at UF; Florida, reprint 2017; St. Photios Greek Orthodox National Shrine, Saint Photios Greek Orthodox National Shrine (stphotios.org).

Adults Only at the Llama Restaurant: Korfhage, Stuart. "St. Augustine restaurant makes top 100 list," *Jacksonville Business Journal*, November 27, 2023; Llama Restaurant.

The Witty Whisker Cat Cafe: Rodriguez, Angeli. *Drinks & Whiskers: How You Can Open a Successful Cat Café*, Independently Published, February 14, 2022; The Witty Whisker Cat Cafe www.wittywhisker.com.

St. Augustine Aquarium: Jones, Colleen. "St. Augustine couple breaks ground on 'dream' aquarium," *Jacksonville Business Journal,* May 30, 2015; Korfhage, Stuart. "St. Augustine Aquarium to be Built on SR 16." *St. Augustine Record,* Dec. 10, 2014; www.saaquarium.com

Nights of Lights in St. Augustine: Nights of Lights, ALL 2024 St. Augustine Nights of Lights Events (visitstaugustine.com); Nights of Lights Questions Answered, Nights of Lights Questions Answered I Visit St. Augustine (visitstaugustine.com).

Old Town Trolley Tours: Historic Tours of America, Historic Tours of America I Ed Swift III; Miller, Mike. *Florida Day Trips*, Adventure Publications, Cambridge, Minnesota, 2020; Old Town Trolley Tours, Buy Discount Tickets Online for St. Augustine Tours and Attractions (trolleytours.com).

Pirate reenactor at
St. Augustine Pirate & Treasure Museum

INDEX

183